# JACKSTRAWS

*The writer thanks The Richmond News Leader
for printing these selections originally
and permitting their publication here.*

Cover design by William Bevilaqua

# JACKSTRAWS

*By*

*Guy Friddell*

THE DIETZ PRESS, INC.  ·  RICHMOND, VIRGINIA
1961

*For Gin and the Boys*

# CONTENTS

# CONTENTS

# CONTENTS

# CONTENTS

# JACKSTRAWS

# DON'T FORGET THE EDELWEISS

What beats me about women is . . .

Their gift for last-minute instructions.

A man is about to embark on a major mission—climbing Mt. Everest, exploring the Congo, or going to the drug store for a quart of ice cream—when his wife appears at the gangplank, calling wildly:

While you're on Mt. Everest, pick up some edelweiss, will you? She wants it for her new hat.

The abominable snowman is an American explorer that got lost looking for edelweiss for his wife.

I was already gunning the motor a week or so ago, going to the corner for ice cream, when my wife flung open the door calling what sounded like: Be sure and bring back a colander.

What kind of picture would you like on the calendar? I roared above the motor.

I said colander, she called.

Listen, I yelled, let's not debate over how to pronounce it. I say to-MAY-to; you say to-MAH-to; I say calendar, you say colander, although I say that's carrying the broad A pretty far.

At that point the lady across the street, Mrs. Gould, called from HER front stoop: What she's trying to tell you is she wants a COLANDER.

(Women stick together that way.)

So she wants a colander, I called back. I'll get a colander with all 12 months, even though we are half-way through the year. But let me suggest that this neighborhood is going unaccountably high hat in calling a calender a colander.

Just forget it, my wife called. I'll use a cocoanut shredder.

If you have learned how to figure the day of the month with a cocoanut shedder, I said, I'm coming in to watch. EVEN EINSTEIN COULDN'T DO THAT.

Never mind, she called. Just get the ice cream and forget the colander.

But you do not tell me lightly to forget a thing. I would still be out there looking for Garcia.

At the drug store I picked out a calendar with a sweet picture of a mother collie nursing her puppies. As I was re-entering the house, remorse struck me. Who am I to let a mere pronunciation create a riffle in the family circle? Calendar . . . colander . . . what's the difference?

I handed it to her, saying (generously), Here's your colander. I'll never understand women.

Do you know she has yet to hang that colander?

---

# THANKSGIVING AT THE SECOND TABLE

One privilege of growing old is you don't have to eat at the second table on Thanksgiving.

Remember? You waited, sunk in the overstuffed sofa in your grandmother's living room along with your 13 cousins and a mud-orange hound dog named Mutt that had slipped in through the cellar entrance and was biting frantically at fleas that weren't there he was so nervous with hunger at all the heavy cooking fragrances that had been seeping out of the big house since dawn.

Relatives, too, had been arriving since dawn, from across town in streetcars and from out in the country over mud roads and timbered bridges. Uncle Ned had driven along one stretch at FOR-TY MILES AN HOUR! Barney Oldfield, we called him.

The city aunts, when they bent to hug you, smelled of perfume and powder. The country aunts had the dry worn look of rocks in an old creek bed and smelled of nothing at all unless it was a faint, acrid whiff of a wood cook stove. I much preferred to be hugged, if at all, by country aunts.

Through the bead-fringed double-doorway leading into the big dining room, as long as a Pullman car, you could hear the mumble and rumble of your elders at dinner. There was a clanking of silverware and an occasional guffaw from your Uncle Bob bent, on a dare from his brothers, on seeing how much he could eat before he exploded like Quilp in Charles Dickens. You could watch him expanding slowly under your eyes. After dinner he would lie, almost in a swoon, on the sofa where you were sitting now, Little Mary Mixup over his face.

Grandmother (who was "Momma" to everybody, even her boys who had reached manhood and had children of their own) was hovering between the kitchen and the dining room. I do not ever recall her sitting down. At this late date it occurs to me to wonder if she EVER sat down—or ATE any of the Thanksgiving dinner.

At Sunday School when the teacher told about Plymouth Rock, the picture of my grandmother always came to the back of my mind, only the rock was a large, comfortable pillow on which you could rest your head, everlasting.

My grandfather, totem pole grim and upright, sat at the head of the table, the provider. He had kept a tight rein on his boys growing up, but nothing tickled him more than to see his grandchildren at odds with his sons. His granite surface would crack into a smile, and he would slyly egg on the third generation.

It was a hardship to wait for the second table—and a pleasure. Time honed such a ravenously thin edge to your appetite that you felt in another minute you wouldn't even be hungry. Then suddenly you were scrambling into the tall dark chair at the table that had taken on an unbelievable number of extra leaves until it appeared as long as a Zeppelin and you couldn't even identify the dishes at the far end.

Your aunts pressed food upon you, solicitous because you had waited for the second table, and, for that reason, even went lightly on the turnips. Each aunt had a dish that was her specialty, a brand name in the family—Ida's dressing, Sarah's potato salad, Dote's pudding—and each competed to see that none of HER dish remained at the end of the dinner. The second table was their last chance. It was like having a coal chute of food open over your head.

The sideboard was laden with tall, stacked, chocolate layer cakes and cocoanut, too, bristling white. There were mince meat pies of volcanic richness and pumpkin pies, round, unblinking and mellow as October suns. Finally, with the table looking like the end of Waterloo, you crept away and went out in the yard with Mutt the dog and threw stones at the back fence and wished you were an explorer on the Amazon living on nothing but quinine bark.

## THE GOLD KNIFE

A friend gave me a tiny gold knife that a boy would probably lose in a week but remember forever.

All day I tried to figure how to give it to one of the three boys in our house short of starting a civil war in which brother would smite brother.

And maybe even father.

Even now I can just hold my own, and when they begin reaching their teens, I think I shall go away to military school.

The knife, a neat novelty, would appeal to the nine-year-old's sense of order, I decided. Anyway, he's nearest the age at which boys can be trusted with knives.

On the other hand, the seven-year-old—now buffer, now bridge between his two brothers— deserved a boost.

I ruled out as too young the five-year-old, a blonde-headed blue jay, always competing, stringbean thin from unceasing effort to match his older brothers. He pokes, nudges, and mocks, trying to cut them to size. At night his legs cramp from churning through the day after them.

Finally, at early supper, with the sun flooding through the back door, I held the knife in my hand, ready to give it to one of the two older boys. They left the table together, and the youngest started to follow. His mother pulled him back for a hug.

He's been a good boy all day, she said.

On impulse, I held out the knife to him. It dangled at the end of the chain, glinting in the sunshine. He made a tiny noise in his throat. An absolutely seraphic smile spread across his face. The smile just hung there, as if it had a life of its own and was going to go on and on, floating about with a boy attached to it.

He took the knife and ran to find his brothers.

The middle boy admired it and then called back to the kitchen, You'll get me one, too, sometime, won't you?

Of course, I said.

The oldest examined the knife, exclaimed over it, and hung

it on the belt loop of the five-year-old. He wore his pants to bed. I counted the day a success.

You so seldom make the right choice, even in as small a thing as a pocket-knife.

---

# WHEN SOUTHERN WOMEN PART

What I need, said my Northern friend, is a guide to Southern talk.

The other day, he said, I was walking from the bus stop with a new neighbor who at parting said, "You all come over." My wife and I switched some plans and went over and, although the visit was most pleasant, it was apparent for just an instant that my neighbor had not expected us to drop in that evening. How can you tell when a Southerner means what he says?

Well, I said, you have asked me a question.

In the South, I went on (still stalling), in the South, talk is moss-hung with kindness and sweet intent. You must not take a Southerner at his word, I added, but on the other hand, you will be making a grievous mistake if you don't.

What the man meant, I said, was that when everything fell out right, when your two wives got to chatting one day at the market, then presently out of the course of time and events, you all would have an evening together.

He didn't mean for you to come barreling over that all-fired instant like a damnyankee. His parting remark was an option on intent, to show you that he liked you and recognized you were friends and hoped you liked him.

But, objected my Northern friend, we had a fine, relaxed evening.

It takes only a moment for a Southerner to adjust a situation to his own slow pace, I replied.

Maybe these manners go back to the days when a few had plantations. Or maybe they arose during Reconstruction when most had nothing and had to dress the day's drab deeds in brave words.

But anyway, I said, you will find that though the talk may seem surface polish, it is heart-felt.

Even when there's nothing to back it up? asked the Northerner.

Most of all, then, I said.

You should listen, I said, to two Southern women talk, to the trailing wisteria vines of conversation that embellish a delicate filagree of meaning. They are the chief custodians of the ritual of conversation, I said. The men might forget but for them.

Have you ever seen two Southern girls greet each other? There are the outcries of recognition, the delicate, pigeon-toed rush to each other's outstretched hands, the gush of conversation. And it is the same, whether they have been separated years . . . or minutes. They try to catch up everything that has happened in the interim, while the men stand by glassy-eyed.

But to see Southern women at their conversational best, I went on, watch them say good-by. At least half the visit is spent on the sweet sorrow of parting.

The women drop graceful adjectives as naturally as a dogwood tree sheds petals. I have known vistors to the South to go about for weeks in a glow from kind compliments extended their dress, looks, and new hair-dos.

In fact, I said, I still have to keep a mental curb on meaning in following my wife's conversation.

What do you mean? asked my friend.

Well, I said, I am sometimes startled to hear her describe as beautiful a person who to me is no more attractive than thousands of us ordinary mortals.

When I tax her on the point, it turns out that beautiful means not only face and figure but also feelings and kindnesses and genuine enjoyment at being with others. It is very confusing, even to a Southerner.

And nice, said the Northerner.

I hope the dissertation wasn't boring, I said, but you asked for it.

Most illuminating, said the Northerner, moving off.

By the way, he added. Let's get together.

Fine, I said. When and where?

Oh, he called, sometime soon. I'll have my wife call yours and they'll fix it up.

# COUGHENSPIELERS

Here the concert season is almost on us and nobody has notified me to get in shape for the first concert.

What do they think—that I could just walk into the hall and start performing without even a warmup? Not even Dizzy Dean could do that.

But I shall be there con gusto (with tie on), tensed to go at the drop of a baton.

You know that magic moment. . . . The house lights dim . . . the orchestra is poised, violins at ready . . . the conductor raises his arms . . . and EVERYBODY BEGINS COUGHING.

The whole house is full of concertspielers.

Down yonder near the pit there's a deep, racking basso profundo who can hardly stay in his seat he's coughing so hard, his head purple with effort to keep on beat . . . and up in the left gallery there's a high, hacking pizzicato.

In the mezzanine there's an accoppitata (full sneeze). . . . Down center somebody is trying a dodecaphonic atonal run, although no one has really been able to do THAT right since Arnold Schonberg. I tend toward a glissando whoop that you do not hear many places outside of Milan.

I have discussed this phenomenon—this compulsion to cough —with some of the leading musicologists here and abroad. None can explain it.

It beats me, said Ferde Grofe.

You don't find it at wrestling matches, political rallies, or circle meetings. Only at concerts. I have my own theory. Nearly everybody, at one time or another, has yearned to play a musical instrument, has wanted to sit down and dumbfound the world with an off-hand andante cantabable.

(I've always wanted to play the glockenspiel, not because I even know what it is, but it would be such a fine, gay thing to say, carelessly, at a party, By the way, I play the glockenspiel.)

Anyway, when the conductor raises his hands, all of us frustrated musicians have an urge to take part, to soar in song, to get into the act—we start coughing.

There is a remedy.

Reserve five minutes before the concert for us coughers—or slap a mustard plaster on everybody as we enter the hall.

---

# SEEING A BOY OFF TO CAMP

He should spend his summer playing on a vacant lot, like I did, I said.

Find a vacant lot in this neighborhood, suggested my wife.

I looked. Sure enough, the vacant lot—the frontier of American boyhood—has gone.

That's how it came about that at the last minute we were putting our child on the train to camp. We packed his foot locker in a store near Main Street Station, right down to the last item on the list—a lock for the foot locker.

Make it a combination lock, I said.

A key lock would be more sensible, said the clerk.

Two things I wanted to do as a boy, I said, explore the Amazon and own a combination lock.

Who's going to camp, you or your boy? asked the clerk.

Well, you're not going, I said.

Nobody's going, said my wife. The train's getting ready to pull out.

The clerk brought the combination lock in a hurry, and I slapped it on the foot locker, first throwing the tag with the formula inside the locker. For safekeeping, I thought.

Look what you did! yelled the clerk. How's he going to open the locker?

A mistake anybody could heve made, I replied. It will provide the counselors with untold amusement on rainy days.

That is, if it gets there at all, said my wife.

We rushed up 20 flights of stairs to the train and put the boy aboard.

Then I leaned in sadness on the red-fudge stone surface of the Main Street Station.

What's the matter? asked my wife.

He and I were so intent on his getting aboard, I didn't give him any parting advice, I said.

You didn't give him the combination to the lock either, said the clerk, who had come along to see off the infernal foot locker.

What do you mean, parting advice? asked my wife

Fathers always give their sons parting advice to look back upon, I said. Stuff like—the friends thou hast, and their adoption tried, grapple them to thy soul with hoops of steel.

But I saw you talking to him at the last minute, said my wife. What were you saying?

I told him, get on the confounded train before it leaves you.

That's not so bad, said my wife. Maybe he won't miss as many trains as you do.

But what will he do without his old dah? I asked.

His what? asked my wife.

His dah, I said. That's dad in Welsh or Scotch or something. You never used it before.

I read it in "How Green Was My Valley," I said. All the children in the valley called their fathers dah. It just came back to me in this moment of stress.

I can just see his first letter to his old dah, I went on.

What does it say? she asked.

Send me an ax to open this foot-locker, said the clerk.

No, I said, just four words: Please come get me.

As a matter of fact it was a week before we heard from him, but there were four words:

Please send fishing pole.

Cryptic, I said.

He wants a fishing pole, she said.

We sent it, and in another week came another letter, also four words:

I caught four fish.

This boy has a grand future in Western Union, I said, but he will never be a newspaperman with such economy of expression.

Thank goodness, said my wife.

You said it, said the clerk.

# FIRST, FIND A WOODEN FREEZER

What we should do on a day like this, I said, is make some old-time home-made ice cream.

Now honestly, asked my wife, how much do you remember about the process?

I remember it clearly as yesterday. One Sunday out of the month your father would get together the parts of the big wooden freezer, borrow some rock salt crystals from next door, and fill the center vat with a rich, egg vanilla custard, pack salt and ice around it in layers, and start cranking. As he cranked away, sweat stood out on his fore-arms and the melting ice ran out of the freezer in little streams down the slanted back porch, streams you could connect with your finger. There was a mockingbird singing out in the peach tree in the hot sun, and when you tried, for fun, to turn the crank, you couldn't.

I liked that bit about the mockingbird, said my wife. You don't find that detail in many recipe books.

You knew the cream was done when it began oozing under the edge of the cap over the vat, and you had to watch sharp, or the family dog, who had come running at the sound of the freezer, would edge in, and take a big lick on the side of the can.

All up and down the street you could hear the grating swirl of turning freezers on back porches or in the shade of big trees. It was a Sunday sound, a happy one, and made up for having to go to church.

And when your father lifted the dasher out of the vat, it was all clumped with ice cream like a snow-laden tree, and you slurped it off the cold metal dasher, leaning over the sink, getting a headache from the ice cream's intense cold. Then he would tamp down the cream in the vat, repack it in ice and salt and wrap it, as I remember, in a big damp towel. It sat on the latticed back porch, in icy, beaded splendor, while you raced through dinner.

Put before you in a bowl, it was like a puffy summer cloud, with a little white rime melting along the rills and edges of the cold, creamy mass, and of such consistency that you could dig a tunnel through it, and gradually whittle at the tunnel with your spoon until at the close you caved it in, and that was that.

That was quite a mouthful, she said, but a little vague in the way of instructions.

I am definitely a big picture man, I said, but we will fill in the details as we go along.

It turned out the details took quite a doing, from finding a freezer, that is in the way of becoming an antique, to running down what the recipe called a "small, common cork," the sort that used to go in castoria bottles. What with the rage for plastic caps, the common cork is most uncommon, I found.

Three hours after the children's bedtime I was still cranking that freezer, wondering what time the ice cream store closed. Occasionally, my wife would spell me, and in phasing out I would have her stand alongside, her hand over mine, turning the crank with me, until suddenly I would shout, NOW! and pull away, calling, DON'T LET IT STOP!

Are you sure all this drama is necessary? she asked, as she took her turn at churning.

Well, I said, walking around swinging my arm to restore the circulation, I have a memory of my grandfather lining up all the uncles to take five-minute stints and when one of them let the crank stop, he would bowl him right off the back porch.

Your turn, said my wife.

We cranked away, until suddenly there was a trickle of ice cream from beneath the cap.

THERE IT IS! I called, like Ahab sighting Moby Dick. THERE IT IS!

We awoke the children, and in tense silence, pulled away the cap. The ice cream stood up in thick, frozen waves.

It's very good, said my wife, as we sat in the kitchen, eating. Does it taste as it used to?

It does and it doesn't, I said. There's something missing. For one thing, $10, even counting the freezer, is a little steep, and further, I don't remember its taking six hours to make, and finally . . .

HEY, LOOK! shouted the middle boy, YOU CAN DIG TUNNELS IN THIS ICE CREAM!

. . . it was worth it, I said.

# BIG WHEEL

It was heigh ho and go to the State Fair with my wife's parting instructions ringing in my ears: Now remember, don't take the children on anything but that nice, safe ferris wheel.

Looking up at it, eight stories high, I wondered if my wife had seen a ferris wheel lately.

The children—my three, a cousin, and a neighbor—were bobbing up and down like the valves on a trumpet playing "Funiculi, Funicula."

Look, I said, why don't we go over there and ride the merry-go-round for tiny tots.

No, no, Funiculi, Funicula, they wanted to go on the big ferris wheel.

We piled in one of the swinging seats and, as the wheel was loading, moving us jerkily toward the top like Br'er Rabbit in the bucket, the middle boy shouted, "Hey, LOOK! This seat don't have no bar across the front to hold onto."

DOESN'T have ANY bar across the front to which to hold, I said, mechanically, reaching for the bar.

HEY! I shouted, IT REALLY DON'T HAVE NO BAR!

But, I said, hastily, don't let that bother you. The old bar is just for show. You're as safe as on the sofa at home. AND DON'T LOOK DOWN. I added, looking down and feeling my stomach turn two Immelmanns.

The wheel stuttered around as people got on, and as we came alongside the operator again, I began to say, diplomatically: I say, old man, if you look I think you'll see that this seat doesn't have any—SWOOSH, with a smooth, sweeping swoop the wheel was carrying us skyward and the ground and clouds were changing places.

EVERYBODY HOLD ON TO GUYBO! I shouted, as well as I could through the folds of the 4-year-old who had wrapped himself vise-like around my neck. Just think what fun we're having, I added.

I tried to brace myself with the right foot and throw the other leg slant-ways across the car as a sort of impromptu bar, rearing back against the seat, praying, called out in a cheery, quavery voice, Mac, Mac, are you holding onto old Guybo's left foot as you should?

The little troupe clung together in frozen silence as the wheel swung up and into that peak where you feel as if the car is going to sail on and out and over into the next county. I distinctly felt all of us, like a mass of seaweed, rise slightly in the seat, and then fall again as we went over the peak and down.

Somewhere, somebody was crying. Was it me? No. Sing a bit. Cheer things up and when you pass that operator get the message to him to let us off, quick.

DID YOUR MO-THER COME FROM IRELAND? I sang, and, passing the rock-eared operator, called in a fast mono-tone. Get - us - off - this - thing. DID SHE WEAR A BONNY SMILE? On and up and over, and everybody was yelling, in fright, including me. Sing, you fool, sing. WILL YOU TELL ME WHERE YOU GOT THOSE IRISH EYES?

By George, I thought, if we ever do get off—and we aren't— I'm going to wrench a bar from another car and pound that fellow in the ground.

I never saw so much ride for the money but finally we were slowing down and then we had stopped, but the earth was still moving and the children were tumbling out, dancing about and saying, Wasn't it FUN? and I wasn't scared A BIT! and Why did your father act so FUNNY? Some kind people helped me out of the car.

Only my youngest was silent, standing, dazed, I thought, gazing up at the wheel.

Poor tyke, I thought. Too frightened to speak. He hadn't said a word the whole time. Just clung to my neck.

I cleared my throat. I could still talk.

What's the matter, Wink? I croaked.

Let's go again, he said.

# THE DAY THE SET CAME

*Ms. found in a picture tube . . .*

As a TV-watcher, I'm a late-comer.

It was three or four years before my father-in-law (after several hints that would have wiped out an atoll) finally got around to giving us a TV set.

Oh, once in a while, going to see friends, I'd had to sit in a darkened room, as if someone were sick, and blink at a lighted postage stamp on the opposite wall. In those early days, I knew one man who was pulled into a darkened living room, told to sit down and shut up, and spent a half hour with a lot of unfamiliar voices before he found he'd walked into the wrong house. The only familiar face was Milton Berle's. When he realized his mistake and tried to apologize to a shadowy circle, he was told just to shut up and get out.

The day our set came I sat down before it around 8 o'clock, intending to get up in about 15 minutes and dismiss the whole thing in a scornful speech. At 4 a.m. I was still stretched out stiff in the big blue chair and ottoman, just my head raised, watching the flickering screen over the horizon that is my tummy. Two neighbors had to come in that morning and unbend me in sections, like a carpenter's rule.

I was a victim of TV-itis.

Our lives narrowed to a little circle around the imitation mahogany metal box, like cavemen huddling over the first fire. We began to talk like cavemen, too, in grunts and barks. Sometimes we'd cut on the lights and try to converse, as in the old days, before TV, but it was a sort of cross-eyed conversation, one eye on the topic, the other on the TV set so as not to miss one of Ted Mack's bright remarks.

What put me on the road to rehabilitation was coming home from work and having to pick my way through the litter of children watching Howdy Doody, children from as far away as across the river. Evenings when the living room was vacant it didn't help me to know that mine were part of a human carpet in somebody else's living room—on the other side of the river. (A child that will not walk 30 feet to supper will go to the North Pole to see Buffalo Bob.)

One evening, I said to my wife, *thismuststop*. I seized the set —it must weigh 80 pounds—and rushed with it to the boys' room in the attic. The children were hardly abed when I tried to wrest it back down again, but it wouldn't budge.

I must have been inspired, I told my wife. I will never touch those heights again.

That night, setless, we sat downstairs in the quietness and ever so often I'd say, "Well, about this time ole Wyatt is walking into a trap a 2-year-old could avoid;" or she'd murmur, "Arthur Murray is waltzing with Katherine about now."

Gradually, we rediscovered life outside the picture screen. The world scene, we found, was larger than 21 inches. I saw that the woman sitting across from me at breakfast was my wife, not Betty Furness or Bess Myerson. She saw that while I was stout, I was not Charlie Chan.

There was a lot of re-learning to go through. I found she liked music. She discovered I pretended to like music, but really liked books. I learned the names and ages of the children again. I realized they were children. and not mousketeers.

We began to talk. Fumblingly, haltingly, at first, just gutturals, but then came words—and whole sentences—and the language began to shine with meaning once more. One evening, while my wife was listening to a symphony on the radio, I picked up a book and, lo, it made sense, as does a quiet old friend to whom you return after a senseless binge.

Friends came in, some of the few who had survived. We gripped each other's hands, strongly, silently. Sometimes we'd talk. Sometimes we'd rest and listen to the silence gratefully, as people in the country used to sit in the summer darkness and listen to katydids and cicadas, a silence unbroken by Ed Sullivan.

Now I can take TV—or leave it, and I usually do when they start churning watches in aquariums, or booming cigaret packs through the air, or singing about cars getting married in the happiest wedding of the year.

I still see a western, now and then. Trouble is, if you cut one on, five stampede into the living room before you can cut it off—

"Gunsmog," "Stuck in the Saddle," "Have Gun, Will Run"—full of fellows that play cards and roll dice and consort with dance hall women, things your wife would scalp you for if you as much as thought of them.

One afternoon, stopping for a hamburger, I found myself sitting beside a fellow I hadn't seen since high school. He saw I was getting fat and bald, and I saw he was getting thin and stooped, mainly from hauling a heavy case of samples in the sun. His face was gray with fatigue. In our talk he mentioned Cheyenne was on that night, and his face brightened a little as we talked of the exploits of those impossibly brave men who walk out into deserted streets and solve their problems with one fast draw.

He finished his hamburger—he had time for only one—and went out. I watched him hurry away, bent over, heading for the next prospect, his feet slapping the hot pavement. Brother, I thought you lose, and lose, and lose, and win just often enough to throw back the wolf.

And you make Cheyenne and all those TV gunslingers look like a sack of creampuffs.

---

# SAVE THE EGGS, ADMONITIONS

The United States Department of Agriculture has published a manual, "Homemakers' Use of and Opinions About Eggs," which notes that two out of every five Americans eat no eggs for breakfast. This calls for a stern reprimand, wasting our money that way and putting two prepositions in a title where one would do, but I don't have it in me to admonish anybody on Monday morning. I can't even look an egg in the eye on Monday.

Anyway, I find the statistics somewhat cheering. I thought I was the only American who ate no eggs for breakfast. Or at least I eat them in a mechanical sort of way, not complaining openly because eggs are the most nutritious food going, and I don't want the children to absorb my prejudice. Robinson Crusoe survived for months on nothing but eggs. That's why he Crusoe.

For some of my friends the day could not begin without an

egg, any more than it could start without the sun. It is a symbol of stability. But there's something about that unblinking yellow orb, full of duty and consistency, that quells me at breakfast. The strange thing is that I enjoy eggs at supper. This bewilders my wife. I tell her privately that I find eggs distressing at breakfast, and then at supper when she serves steak, I ask: Why don't we ever have eggs for supper around here? What have you got against eggs?

I have always had a hankering for steak for breakfast. A small steak. I'm not greedy. Oh, you might as well throw in the gravy, too, and lots of it, while you're about it, and maybe some hot biscuits, and it's as easy to make a panful as a few, so don't spare the dough, and a dab of damsons or two, and a wedge of country butter, and plenty of hot coffee. But no cream. I have to watch my weight.

Economists would object that steak for breakfase is too expensive, but is it any more expensive—and I ask you this in all honesty —is it any more expensive at breakfast than it is at supper?

Maybe it's the monotony that makes me shrink from eggs at breakfast. That must be, because invariably on a train trip I order eggs for breakfast and find them exotic amid the changing scenery and the swaying car.

Just turn the confounded menu around, I told my wife the other morning. Start cooking breakfast at supper and supper at breakfast. Change the clock, if necessary. Let's cut out all this conformity. Use some imagination. Show some daring.

So you know what we had this morning? Turnip greens.

---

# GOING BACK

My wife's high school class of 1941 held its 20-year reunion and even outdrew the reunion of my class of 1939, although ours did inspire theirs. Later, going home, I told her: It's just like Picasso said: You do a thing first, and somebody comes along and does it pretty.

The '41 reunion did give me a chance to watch more clearly

what was going on.  Two years ago, for the class of '39, I stepped blithely, unwittingly, back into time, and, at the first sight of an old classmate, the girl who sat by me in Plane Geometry, fell into a frozen trance.  The past, present, and future kept intermingling, like a school of happy, unruly porpoises, and all evening I felt on the verge of some great utterance, something like Einstein's theory of relativity as applied to high school reunions, but only sat, stunned, with a tiny, tight smile on my fat Mona Lisa face, loving everybody, saying nothing, so that near the end, going out, I heard one class-mate mutter to another: There goes Friddell, an even bigger jerk than he was in T-J, if that's possible.

Saturday night I was able to appreciate the look of dismay that spread across the face of others when they stepped across the threshold of the Winter Garden and saw a throng of people made up as if they were old friends playing the role of adults in the Senior Class play or utter strangers, imposters, trying to pass themselves off as somebody long gone.  The boys, generally, were the most difficult to recognize because they had widened considerably, or lost their hair, or both.  As for the girls the most frequent observation from the men was: What was wrong with my eyesight back in '41?

The teachers had changed the least.  Nearly everything in life suffers a shrinking in time's rinse.  To go back to an old neighborhood and look at the houses, the trees, is like peering through the wrong end of a telescope.  Everything's smaller.  But, I've found, teachers never undergo this loss of stature.  In fact, they tend to become larger with time, perhaps because they are always in touch with the future.

You think back, and the clearest thing you can recall usually, about each year of your life, is the image of your teacher, the landmarks of our days.  They never fall in your estimation.  Indeed, in their presence, YOU tend to feel small, because THEY know what's behind the front.  Somehow teachers have found a way to beat time, which is why, I guess, the state politicians feel it unnecessary to pay them much.  The teachers have their reward in having trained the politicians, and the rest of us.

The class of '41 sang the school fight song (from which "On Wisconsin" was stolen) and the Alma Mater (with everybody coming through strongly on "Thou hast taught us how to live.").

Then, seeing that my wife was having a good time, running from person to person with cries of delight, I wandered out into the corridor where I bumped into three of the youngest people I had ever seen, high school journalism students sent to study us, it turned out. For a moment though, I thought they were of the class of '41, and, indeed, had started to bellow: GOOD TO SEE YOU AGAIN! until I realized, Careful now . . . NOBODY is going to look this young after 20 years.

Things settled into focus, and, as we chatted, I asked what had impressed them most about us. They hesitated, and then, seeing as the four of us were colleagues, in a sense, they broke down:

"You sing the school fight song so much more slowly . . . . so that we could even understand the words . . . You know . . . there's no (a girl doubled her fist and struck it into her palm) . . . Another thing . . . you wait a LONG-G-G time to laugh after the jokes . . . Everything seems, somehow, I don't know . . . SLOW-ER . . ."

I nodded, numbly, thanked them, and went back inside, feeling like Dorian Gray on the point of dissolution. My wife was talking to the fellow that took her to the Junior-Senior Prom, still disgustingly handsome. She spun around at my tap on her shoulder, her eyes shining, and, seeing me, a tiny frown came between her eyes, as if, I thought, she couldn't quite place the fat slob standing before her, a blend of The Three Stooges

There's a strange look on your face, she said. Is something wrong?

Yes, I said. Time.

---

# NOTES FROM AN OLD BASSOON

The other evening my wife took a chance and took me to a musicale at a friend's home. Now behave, she said, as I was ringing the doorbell, resisting an impulse to play shave-and-a-hair-cut-two-bits on the chimes.

Don't worry, I replied. When it comes to music, I'm a regular bassoon.

Remember your age, she was saying, just as the door was opening so that when the hostess asked, How are you? I said, 39.

That is, pretty fine, I said, recovering nimbly I thought.

Inside, the guests were seated, feet together, hands on knees as if strapped for a rocket shot to the moon. A lawyer friend, usually exuberant, looked as if he had been cast in wax.

The evening proved surprisingly good fun. The pianist, even I could tell, was splendid. Only one thing bothered me. Where do you LOOK when listening to music in company?

First I glanced at my lawyer friend, who doesn't know the first two words of Yankee Doodle. That almost broke me up, the sight of him, and so I frowned and stared at the tip of my left shoe.

Scuffed, I saw. I thrust it underneath the chair and stuck out the right shoe.

Strange. A white smear across that toe. Paint, perhaps? Lard?

I thought of passing a note to my wife across the room: Honey, how in the world could I have got lard on the toe of my shoe?

But I couldn't find a pencil. Just as well. She probably wouldn't have answered anyway. She was lost in the music. A vacation from Friddell, poor dear.

I tried staring, severely, at the corner of a curtain rod and, after a few seconds, found I couldn't look away.

By George, I thought, I've hypnotized myself. What a hullabaloo when THIS is discovered. The hostess snapping fingers in front of my eyes, the lawyer pouring water over my head. He WOULD do that.

Fortunately, about that time I recognized an old friend in the music itself. The pianist was playing a Russian piece, The Gate at Kiev, and like so much that is Slavic (he said later), it was filled with excitement and lots of bells.

Suddenly, plain as daybreak, I heard, tinkling through all the tumbling notes: Morn-ing bells are RING-ing. Over and over I heard it.

The music ended, and I jumped up, shouting, Morning bells are ringing! I heard it! I heard it! Plain as day!

What do you mean, morning bells are ringing? asked the lawyer, looking around for the water pitcher.

You remember, I said.  It goes like this, I added (singing) :
Are you slee-PING?  Are you slee-PING?
     Bro-ther John?  Bro-ther John?
Morn-ing bells are RING-ing, morn-ing bells are RING-ing . . .
     Ding dong DING, ding dong DING . . .
Are you slee-PING?  Are you slee—
That's enough, said the lawyer.  We get the idea.

The pianist, a good joe, smoothed everything over with a quick dissertation on bells in music, and everybody forgot my spontaneous contribution.

Nearly everybody.

Did you HAVE to sing? asked my wife, as we drove home.

Well, I said, it WAS a musicale, wasn't it?

---

# WHAT ALOHA MEANS TO ME

The Senator from Hawaii suggested that Congress put a statue of Robert E. Lee in Washington, a replica of the one in Richmond on our Monument Avenue.  This pleased me, even more so because our Virginia Congressmen, along with the rest from Dixie, had opposed Hawaii's coming into the Union.

That is the Aloha spirit.

There are a dozen nationalities in those islands—Hawaiians, Filipinos, Japanese, Chinese, and so on—but they are united by a gentility that made itself felt from the moment my crazy outfit stepped—or fell—off the ship in Honolulu during World War II.

The rumor had been that we were going to Alaska because, just before we embarked from San Francisco, the crafty Army had issued us heavy woolen uniforms, including a mustard-colored overcoat that would have swallowed a horse.

When the ship finally stopped, nobody down in the bowels with us knew where we were until word drifted down that there were hula girls outside.

Along with the overcoat, each man wore his dress wool uniform, including his steel helmet, and was draped with a gas mask, a musette bag, and a carbine but no ammunition because even the Army had more sense then THAT.  Every man carried, too, a pair of green barracks bags, packed to the bursting point, weighing about 60 pounds each. You carried them tied together, yoked over a shoulder, one fore and the other aft so that when the front one swayed into your knees and almost threw you backwards, the other came swinging from behind and pitched you forward again.

We like never to have got out of the hold. Almost at the top of the ship's ladder, some poor failing soul would lose his grip on the rungs, and, shouting, LOOK OUT BE-LOW-W-W-W-W, come piling down, pulling everybody with him.

We would lie there, panting, until Sergeant Maypop would yell: ALL RIGHT, YOUSE GUYS, IF YOU WANT TO SEE THOSE HULA GIRLS, GET UP AND START CLIMBING AGAIN.

By degrees we got out on deck, where the sun hit us like a fist in those wool uniforms, and then down to the dock where nobody could have raised his head to look at the hula girls, even if they had been there.

There was a walk of a mile through downtown Honolulu to a little pineapple train of waiting freight cars. Every 20 feet we would fall in a sweating heap in the street and then jerk forward again, a wavering, spasmodic, twitching line of men, like a snake dying in the sun.

At one point, bent double and too tired to lift the helmet off my eyes, I staggered off at a right angle from the others until I heard Sergeant Maypop yelling, dimly, somewhere: FRIDDELL, YOU MAD FOOL, YOUSE ARE RUNNING A RED LIGHT!

About that time my back lightened magically as the weight of the barracks bags was lifted from my shoulders. I looked up. There, smiling at me, was the fattest man in the loudest shirt I had ever seen. The squat, tan Hawaiian, bearing the barracks bags, fell in step with me, steadying me with his hand, and walked beside me to the freight car.

It was happening all up and down the line as smiling, impromptu porters appeared from shops and even out of cars stopping alongside us.

That was how we came into Hawaii.

That's why I was happy to hear Hawaii had come into the United States.

Aloha, Hawaii!

# KITCHENWARE IS MOVING WELL

I guess, conservatively, that I have sold about $250,000 worth of goods this Christmas.

Without getting a cent for it.

There's something—I don't know what—that makes people come up and place orders with me.

Kitchenware is moving very well this year.

Much better than last, when I didn't sell a single rubberized dish rack.

Copper moulds are big . . . the kind in the shapes of the Capitol dome, or a cluster of grapes, or a big fish swimming along with a a sulky under-lip.

If you want to surprise your husband, I told one lady, just fill that tin fish with a tuna casserole and see what he says.

(That's something else I can't explain . . . why women think men like tuna casserole. THEY don't eat it. All they do is serve it and beam.)

I think I should have been a clerk. Even the clerks mistake me for one of them.

Oh, Mr. Slemp said one of them (the name on her placard, I saw, was Miss Tingledell), as I was cutting through the store to get out of the rain for a block, Oh, Mr. Slemp, we are running out of handkerchiefs over on counter nine.

Take mine, I said, generously.

Perhaps the mistake comes about because I usually nip in and out of the stores on my lunch hour, without a hat or coat. Perhaps it's my attitude that makes people think I'm minding the store, a sort of don't care air all clerks have to adopt around Christmas, if they are to survive.

Nothing is so wearing as a walk through milling aisles of shoppers. The newspapers don't help, printing those grim reminders— only so many more shopping days for Santa. Anyway, when persons in this frenzied state seek help, it's safer to try and direct them than go into an involved explanation of where you work. They're not interested in THAT.

Just the other day a lady asked me where the didoo dolls were and her husband in tow, said Hon, he doesn't work here . . . Hon, he doesn't work here, and when I said that indeed, he was right I didn't work there, she turned on her husband, and in a loud voice, said Why didn't he say he didn't work here?

I try to help in self-defense.

A mother approached yesterday, holding a gun and belt out before her, and said to me, without even so much as a hello, Whatever in the world am I going to do? My little boy is left-handed and can't draw from a right-handed holster.

Madam, I said, go swap it for a two-gun belt.

However can I thank you? she said.

Don't try, I said. That's what I'm here for.

Sometimes though I'm stumped

As I was passing through umbrellas, a lady with a face as set as a skillet, rushed up and said, Young man, where can I buy a top that whistles six tunes?

Madam, I said, if you find out, I wish you'd tell me.

Well, she said, relaxing a little, that's a funny answer.

I'm glad you think so, I said, for it's all meant in the spirit of Christmas.

A Merry Christmas to you, she said, moving away more leisurely.

And a year full of happy top tunes to you, I called after her.

What I can't understand is why I haven't received so much as a thank you from the stores.

---

# A SILVER FISH IN THE SINK

Wake up, said the voice at my ear. Wake up, and see what I caught.

There, within about three inches of my nose, was a grimy hand holding a package, not as large as a deck of cards, wrapped in wax paper.

It's a fish, said the voice of the 6-year-old.

What sort of fish? I asked, fighting for time.

A "brim."

Where'd you catch it?

In the water.

No, I mean where'd you catch it from?

The end of a line.

No, I mean where were you standing when you caught it?

On the edge.

You mean you caught that by yourself?

I caught part of it.

No point in continuing along this line. Just better accept that fish, and let it go at that. And the sooner it goes, the better. But work at that part carefully for you can see he's attached to that fish.

What are you going to do with it?

Eat it.

It's too small. How big is it, inside that paper?

Three or four inches. Probaly five.

Listen . . . I'll tell you what. It's too small to eat. Do like the Indians. Plant it, with a flower.

A LIVE fish!

YOU MEAN THAT'S A LIVE FISH? I moved my face back a foot.

Whaddaya think?

Let's get him out of here.

This is the quiet one, the middle boy, the sharer in a pack of cannibals, the dogged helper in raking leaves, but now his face assumed a mulish expression you associate with stories of the Emperor Tiberius.

No, he said, I'm going to keep it.

You better put it in some water then. Put it in the bathroom sink while we think this thing out.

In the sink the fish floated on its side, limply.

He's dead, I said.

No, said the boy. He's alive.

The gills moved slightly in the glistening sides, the bream righted itself, and in another five minutes was sailing about the sink in bold plunging lines, an inspiring sight. We watched for a while, then cut off the light, at his suggestion, and went to look for a container outside.

The boy's mother waved to us gaily as she entered the house.

In a moment there came a stifled shriek.  Right off I knew she had discovered the fish.  She stood on the back stoop, pointed dramatically, and called to us:  There's a fish in the bathroom sink!

NO!  I said.  THERE COULDN'T BE!

Yes, a fish, a silver fish.

BY GEORGE, I shouted, THIS IS TOO MUCH!  ONLY SIX MONTHS IN THIS HOUSE AND ALREADY WE'VE GOT SILVERFISH.  CALL THAT CONFOUNDED CONTRACTOR!

It's a fish of the fin variety, she said, acid etching her tones, and you know it.

It must have come up through the pipes, I said.  That's what it is.  It's spawning time in the James, and this heroic fish has climbed all the way into our sink.  What a wonderful thing Nature is, after all.

Either the fish goes, she said, or I go.

I looked at the boy.  It was his choice.

We got in the car and found a lake and he up-ended the pitcher, and the fish disappeared almost immediately into the coffee-brown waters, I thought.

I saw it wave, he said.  He's wondering if he's back in the sink, and he's going all around the edges of the lake to find out.

You've done a great thing, I said.  You have given a wild thing its freedom.

Yes, he said, and next year we will come back and catch it again.

We drove home, in fairly good shape, and there was my wife waiting on the back stoop.

Go in and talk to your oldest.  He has something to show you.

Listen, I said, don't give me bad news in bits and pieces.  What is it?

A dead mole.  He insists he's going to carry it to school for 'Tell and Show.'  He's getting ready to stuff it, and I can't stop him.

I braced my shoulders. Who said modern life was dull and predictable?

# PASS THE POTTAGE, PLEASE

There's a conspiracy among doctors, wives, and dietitians to banish from the dinner table what some of us call salt pork and others term fat-back or streaker-lean-streaker-fat or sidemeat bacon, and nearly all of us grew up on.

Now I am no doctor (this admission will come as a vast surprise to some of my friends who were under the impression that I had interned at Glasgow with Glendenning) but I can't believe that any harm comes from a smidgin of salt pork, a mere afterthought, dropped into a pot of vegetables.

The tang of salt pork, used with discretion, is a part of Southern cooking, and if the AMA is going to attack THAT, then it can just count me out of the fight against socialized medicine.

Salt pork gives vegetables a sort of environment in which to work around and get to know each other. It invokes a spirit of togetherness.

Take string beans, or snaps, or whatever you care to call them. Cooked as is, with no salt pork to introduce one bean to another and blend things, snaps are stand-offish and well-nigh inedible. They just don't mesh. I would as soon try to eat a pot of boiled shoe strings or new clothes pins.

But a big pot of snaps on the back of the stove, simmering in the benign fission of salt pork, with four or five large potatoes gradually turning the tan hue of Octagon soap and taking on the flavor of the salt meat through and through, then served with several large slices of vinegar-soaked Bermuda onion cut up in the beans, a wedge of hot, buttered cornbread alongside—there is a dish that has verve.

In my youth the Sunday School teacher used to tell of one brother selling the other his birthright for a mess of pottage.

I couldn't keep the brothers apart and wasn't sure what the birthright was, but I had a clear picture of the pottage as a big pot, blackened on the bottom and filled with string beans cooked a long time in streaker-lean-streaker-fat.

I didn't think it was such a bad trade.

# TRIPLE EXPOSURE

It's Richmond Day, said my wife, gleefully, as if it were Christmas. Why don't you buy a sport coat?

Because, I said, the merchants have not reached that state of beneficence where they are giving away clothes.

(Actually, it's not a lack of money that bothers me. I have so much money that I do not have time to count it, or pay my bills. Look, I say to those people who keep writing letters at the end of the month: You better be careful, or I'll get together all my money —from out of last year's Summer suits, from under the sofa cushions, the middle boy's piggy bank, the deposits on the soft drink bottles—AND COME DOWN THERE AND BUY YOU OUT. Then where will you be?

(On easy street, says the store manager. This account goes back eight years.)

No, if I had a million dollars, I'd still be loath to buy a sport coat. It's those three-way mirrors.

Over the months a fellow gets used to seeing himself head on as he shaves or steals a glance in passing at his reflection in a plate glass window. Not so bad, he thinks. A little bit of the fathead, here and there. A double chin or two. The old waistline is on the march, and the hair is on the retreat. But get by all that and there's a touch there of—well, I don't know what—but there definitely is a touch there, of something.

Then one day, on lunch hour, you drop into a store, drawn by a sale, step smartly into the little mirror alcove near the suit racks, and it's like being tripped, kicked and slapped in one operation. You stand there, dazed. Who is that near human, looking at me so insistently, so strangely? you think. Who is that dropsical pelican trying to ruin this store with his presence? Who is that standing there transfixed in gargoyle ugliness?

Face it. There's no way out. It's me.

At this point in my breakfast reverie, there was an interruption. I know what you're thinking, said my wife, who majored in mind-reading in school. I know you're worrying about seeing yourself as others see you. Brace up, she said. Be a sport. You're every bit as good as that old three-faced mirror, and don't you forget it.

Sure I said, weakly. Chins up.

That's how it came about that on Richmond Day I stood before the three-fold mirror draped in a hounds-tooth sports coat and a clerk.

A handsome fit, if I ever saw one, said the clerk.

I never saw a worse one, I said, gazing at the face.

(The man of a thousand faces, I thought, all of them ugly.)

Now. said the clerk, flitting around me like a darning needle, I think we can just take this up a pinch in the middle, and it'll do wonders.

How can man change what God hath wrought? I asked.

Oh, come, he said, it's not that much of a project. A stitch in time, you know.

No, No, I said, still gazing at the face that would start a clock in terror. No, I'll leave it as it is, thank you.

Shall I wrap it? he asked.

I wish you could, I said. I wish you could wrap it and drop it over there in that box of trash. But I guess I'll have to take it with me. As is.

I walked, weak-kneed, toward the busy street, and, walking across the plush carpet, I felt I was leaving something, someone behind. I glanced back.

The ugly apparition was gone, probably melted back into the triple exposure. Good riddance, I thought, gazing, smiling, in the nearest flat, plate glass window.

---

# TRICK OR TREAT?

The first Halloween in a new neighborhood all three boys had colds and couldn't go out. A blessing, I thought, but their mother said to me: Why don't you dress up as a ghost and go across the street where they can watch you from the window and trick and treat for them?

Listen, I said, I might consent to go over there and ring the doorbell, but if I do, leave the front door open because I am going to run faster than you have ever seen me run. I will be back over here before the bell stops ringing over there.

Oh, be a sport, she said.

I am a sport, I said. I am the only adult in town who is going up and ring a front door bell and run WHILE HIS CHILDREN SIT BACK AND WATCH.

You'll love the Goulds, my wife promised.

No I won't, I said. Not until I meet them next Summer.

She draped and pinned me in an old sheet and placed on my head a woman's straw hat, last year's bird nest in navy blue, and poked a can of shaving cream in my face.

Why are you pointing that shaving cream in my face? I asked, suspiciously.

F-S-S-S-S-S-S-T-T-T-T-T-T!

Right in the old kisser.

Honey, I said, that last trick would be grounds for divorce if I weren't sure no jury would ever believe it.

They guided me out the door, on a diagonal course toward the Goulds. Weaving across the lawn, I tripped over the sprinkler.

Don't show off, she called. Just play it straight.

I wavered over to the Goulds' lighted stoop, and, setting my feet for a fast get-away, reached out to ring the bell when the door opened, and there was Mr. Gould.

A big guy. Probably could run 100 yards in 10 seconds, I thought. He'd catch me before I got out of the yard. Play the thing cool. You've been in more embarrassing spots than this. Lots and lots of 'em. Though I don't remember when. Carry it off lightly.

Hello, I said through the shaving cream. I'm your neighbor from over the way. Thought I'd drop by and say hello. First chance since we moved in, you know. Spirit of the season and all that. That explains this informal garb.

(In a flash I'd discarded that sock and bull story about the three sick children. I didn't even believe it myself any more.)

Sure, sure, sure, Mr. Gould was saying all the time I was talking. Come right in, he said, steadily backing away. Marilyn, he called, come in and meet Mr. Friddell from across the street. Come quickly.

Mrs. Gould came in, paused a fraction of an instant, and I will hand it to her that after a second, in which her eyebrows flew up like window shades, she was a gracious hostess. Mr. Gould sat over in the corner and stared in disbelief.

Well, I said, after I had sat down, I've got to be running along. Where's my hat?

I looked around. The old bird's nest had vanished, and I didn't blame it.

Half blindfolded by the sheet, as if incarcerated in a tank, I could only see about 15 degrees of the room. Figuring I'd dropped it, I got down on all fours, patting the floor around me. Mr. Gould joined me.

It's on your head, said Mrs. Gould.

I staggered for the doorway, and she put a sack of bubble gum and lollipops in my hand.

For your boys, she said.

Back home, several thousand miles across the street, the children bounced around like peeper frogs and divided the bubble gum.

How ever did you do it? asked my wife, clasping her hands. I'd have been scared to death.

You have a thing to do, and you do it, I said. That's all.

## BLOW-TOAD

For years now people have been calling me a big blow-toad, and only the other day I saw one at the beach. It's the one homeliest animal—or fish—I ever saw. I have a theory as to how the blow-toad came about. The Lord had put in a busy day in the Garden of Eden, forming this and that plant and animal, and was standing, with a handful of mud, looking around, wondering how it would all look to Him in the morning, and He let the mud sort of dribble out of His hand onto the ground and then strode out of the Garden. The mud commenced to wiggle, the first blow-toad.

The blow-toad is a muddy-colored fish about as big as a stick of butter. When it is excited, its white belly swells into a volley-ball. The first I saw came at the end of a haul by a seine boat when the teen-agers in the crew began tossing blow-toads to the waiting children on the beach.

The air was filled with the globular creatures, like flying pigs from Alice in Wonderland. When they hit the beach, they bounced with a smart, spanking noise. My three boys watched in awed envy, until a boy everybody had been calling Bucket thrust one of the fish in their hands. Here, he said.

In a frenzy they got a tin lunch box out of the car, filled it with water, plopped the blow-toad inside and then exhorted me to drive faster, faster to the cottage where we were staying before the water ran out. If a cop stopped us, I had a great explanation all ready: I am hurrying to save the life of a blow-toad, Officer.

The boys spent the rest of the day constructing at the water's edge a vast system of pools and dikes in which the blow- toad swam.

Near the end, assured by them that it wouldn't bite, I picked it up for a closer look. Even a blow-toad, I saw, has points of beauty.

Its round, shirt-button eyes shifted, as I turned it about, from light amber to deep azure, as full of colors as the sea itself. Let's turn it loose, I suggested.

They nodded, and the middle boy placed it at the shallow shore line. The blow-toad moved about a yard in one direction, then cut more swiftly to the other side, testing its boundaries, and then headed straight out until he faded into the shadowy depths of deep water.

---

# HI FI ON THE LO' FLO'

At a gathering the other evening suddenly everybody was sitting on the floor with their shoes off listening to classical music on the stereo.

Everybody but me.

I leaned against the door jamb. Casually, I hoped.

Must you ALWAYS be different? whispered my wife. Please sit down.

In THIS suit? I shot back. Nothing doing. This is my

Sunday suit in which I apply for jobs, interview big shots, and go to Sunday school. It is not for playing in sandpiles or sitting on floors.

I'll never understand you, said my wife. If the rest were standing, you'd be sitting on the floor with your shoes off.

In this suit, I said, I would not sit on the floor with Eisenhower.

Or Stevenson, I added, in the interest of any old-line Democrats present.

Oh, for goodness sakes, said my wife.

Not even with Kennedy, I went on, but I want it CLEARLY UNDERSTOOD that it would have nothing to do with his religion.

Please forget it, she said.

I WILL take off my shoes, I offered, although there's a toehole in one sock.

Just be still, she said, and let the others enjoy the Warsaw Concerto.

Presently, I did compromise. I hunkered down on the floor Indian-like, arms across knees, hands supporting chin.

As kids we would sit around the old campfire for hours that way and then spring into a war dance.

Abruptly I realized I could no longer jump into a war dance from a hunkered down position.

I could not even get up.

The old legs go first as they say in boxing.

By George, I thought, this IS a dilemma. Can't get up. Can't sit down.

I found though that I could sway slightly from side to side, like a sick elephant, and that's what I was doing, readying for a tremendous takeoff effort when suddenly I swayed too far in one direction and went over sideways with a resounding crash.

EXACTLY at that point in the symphony when the Poles were firing cannon, ringing bells, tearing down barricades, or whatever it is Poles do when they are upset.

Boom-tiddy-boom-tiddy-boom-boom—KERRASH!

It brought everybody back from Warsaw to Richmond with a BANG.

My head hit a gate-leg table, which I have always considered a monstrosity anyway.

GIVE HIM AIR, somebody shouted.

What happened? everybody was asking.
It was that wild, wild music, I said.
He is a true lover of good music, somebody murmured.
That seemed to satisfy everyone.
Except my wife.
Honestly, she said, as we drove home.

---

# FALL GUYS

This is the time of year to beware, the Fall.

Not the Spring, with her haunting lassitude.

In the Spring, just before a man's heart breaks . . . he goes to sleep.

Nor the Summer, with his roaring, blazing laughter. You know where you stand with the Summer.

And certainly not gnarled, pinch-cheeked Winter, the season to burrow inside furs and houses. Just a touch of Winter is enough to make a man wonder why he complained of the humidity in July.

The Winter is best felt second-hand. A child runs to greet her mother, and, pressing against her, feels the cold draughts still clinging inside the folds of her coat.

Autumn combines them all, the wrap-up. The ghosts of all the seasons walk the land. There's a final flare of Summer, the last splash of precious sunshine, that has warm, golden tints you don't see in the white-hot intensity of July and August. There's a melancholy tinge of Spring, too, in the light breezes over a green hill against picture-puzzle clouds. And there's just a flick of Winter's whip to put a tonic in the blood.

A person feels he or she can do the impossible.

Boys go out for football, the movie of the 80-yard game-winning run turning constantly in their minds. Men start long books, set out to break 80 for the first time in their lives, commit themselves, rashly, to another installment plan, launch construction projects that end, when Winter strikes, as tumbling markers to good intentions. Women join clubs, organize vast, complicated car pools, or try to bottle the season in rich, dark Mason jars, become enmeshed in schedules that plague them the rest of the year. Children set off, soaring, to school, bent on putting another red or blue star on reading lists. Young girls debate the choice of a sweater-skirt combination to match the season's vivid promise.

Autumn cart-wheels on stage in a flashing carnival of colors, motley Harlequin in red, yellow, orange and green.

A laughing magician, whose sleight of hand poses a warm, somnolent Summer day when a man's trying his dogged best to follow the sermon in church—and a cold, wintry drizzle when he sets off, light-footed, to the football game.

It's a gay, feverish-cheeked season of contrasts . . . drifting brown leaves. gleaming chrome of new model cars . . . cheer-leaders in trout-like leaps against gray stadium stands . . . dry shocks of harvest corn, the orange glow of pumpkins, fat epitomes of the time of year.

Winter waits around the corner with his frozen breath, the dark months lightened only by the Christmas tree glowing at the end of the year's long corridor.

Winter? Never heard of it. It doesn't exist.

Don't talk to me about dull Winter.

Just now, I'm a grasshopper, fiddling, dancing in the sun.

For now, we're all Fall guys.

---

## SANTA PSYCHOANALYZED

"Would you ever have thought of Santa Claus as a sex symbol?"

WOULD I WHAT? I shouted, jumping up, looking around wildly to see that none of the children were near.

That's what it asks right here in the paper, said my wife. The story quotes a Dutch psychologist on a year's leave of absence from the Center of Advanced Study in Palo Alto, Calif.

On a year's leave of absence from his senses, you mean, I said. The paper ought to be careful about printing stuff like that. Sure, sure, it's a free press, but let us not forget, ladies and gentlemen, that with that freedom goes responsibility and—

Sit down, said my wife. You're out of breath.

It goes on to say, she went on, that modern studies of numerous legends have found that, apart from his interest in children, there is evidence of this other.

Oh, well, I said, if you're going to rule out the main reason for his being—his devotion to children—then you can say ANYTHING about Santa Claus. For instance, look what's done to him in advertising. Everywhere I go these days I see him stealing soft drinks on billboards.

Santa has survived it all, Somehow, despite the hucksters, despite the myth-breakers, the big, red-suited fellow goes on year after-year, the image as clear as ice, tip -toeing like an elephant through daisies, bent on doing good as if it were mischief.

There the picture is, I said, a chance for grown-ups at the close of a long, mostly frustrating year, to pause and create for children a shimmering fantasy, a little world that sparkles like a Christmas bauble. On that one day, every man and woman is a poet. The picture is SO clear that you might know that one day some psychiatrist would find it necessary to get hold of Santa. What I wonder is, HOW DID HE MANAGE TO KETCH HIM when children tried for years and failed?

Each Christmas you steeled yourself against sleep. Then the next instant you were awake, and it was morning, or pretty nearly so, and you dashed to the living room, almost in time to catch a presence of something, a lingering redness maybe from his coat, Then the toys and tree flooded your sight, and the old elf had slipped away again. Once, half-waking, I heard a faint wash of sleigh bells, as of a door opening an instant on merriment far off. That, I think, was the closest I got to Santa.

I wish I'd been present at the interview with the psychologist. I wonder did he give Santa an aptitude test, such as you're put through when you apply for a new job.

Mr. Claus, says the interviewer, leaning forward in his chair, Do you like PEOPLE?

Well, yes, I'd say so, says Santa, and about that time he hears Blitzen pawing the snow outside, and he adds, brightening, But I like reindeer, too. Most of all. though, he goes on, defensively, I like children.

The psychologist scribbles something on a scorecard and then he says: Now, Mr. Claus, do you have a negative or positive attitude on life? Are you of a go-giving or a retiring nature?

I sure don't like much to be caught, admits Santa.

Now, says the psychologist, we're going to give you the ink-blot test. Just drop this bit of ink on the blotter . . . That's-s-s-s right . . . Now what does that remind you of? What do you see?

What I see, says Santa, is the face of a child turned to the sky, looking for me, so I'll have to leave you now, and quickly.

---

## THE TWA CORBINES

Marine General "Chesty" Puller roared his scorn at the Army's recent decision to swap rifles for lighter carbines.

"CORBINES," he called them . . . as if they were some disreputable species of crow-like scavengers.

I never cared for a carbine myself. It was a buzzard to take apart and put togther.

The army was leery of issuing my outfit carbines—or anything that would go off.

It was a strange outfit, a medical unit made up of castoffs from draft boards all over the United States  In most outfits, a man as old as 35 was automatically "Pop." In ours, he was "Kid."

Although we were a concentration of short-comings, we had a pride as fierce as that of the three musketeers . . . twenty years after.

When Sergeant Maypop issued us carbines, he told us flatly we could never, never shoot at the enemy, under the Geneva rules governing medics.

If you do, he warned, I'll lose my stripes.

Before any of us went on guard duty, he always removed our carbines, like a mother taking a sling-shot from her youngster's back pocket.

Walk softly and carry a big stick, said Sergeant Maypop.

He never had to remove my carbine.

I took it apart once and never got it together again. There was always one piece missing—or one too many. Finally, I piled all the odds and ends in a tent shelter-half and took them to the sergeant.

I'm turning in these car bones, I said.

Why? he shouted.

I can't make them come out even, I said.

I think it was made in Japan, I added.

What he said was unprintable, not because it was profane, but you just can't put a bellow on paper.

Take that mess out of here, and get it together for the big review, he ordered.

Not long after, one of my friends came to my tent with a long, flat package.

He was one of the finest men I ever met, a master carpenter, so good at whittling that we called him Geppeto.

Open the package, he said.

Inside was a wood facsimile of a carbine, right down to the last millimeter. He had carved it perfectly. Best of all, it had only two parts—a barrel and a stock.

Now open this, said my friend, handing me an identical package.

In it was a second wooden gun carved in two parts, but this one was painted artfully with sun-shiny highlights all along the gleaming barrel.

It made your eyes blink.

The dull carbine is for gray, overcast days, my friend explained. The bright one is for sunshine.

That's how he was.

A perfectionist.

And a humanitarian.

The day of the big review dawned clear and sunny so I took the shiny wood version of the carbine to the parade ground. As the parade formed, one of those quick Hawaiian squalls darkened the sky.

Just as my platoon approached the reviewing stand there was a gray downpour that made it look as if we were struggling in the folds of a curtain. Above the pounding rain we heard the voice of our commander, the only man in the Central Pacific with more lung power than Sergeant Maypop.

SERGEANT, he roared, THAT MAN OUT THERE HAS A GUN THAT'S SPARKLING EVEN IN THE MIDST OF

ALL THIS RAIN. SEE THAT HE'S PROMOTED ONE
DEGREE IN GRADE.

That's how I attained the highest rank of my military career.
Pfc.

I know, I know, Pfc is automatic now after six monuths.

Back there you had to earn it.

---

# SNOWBOAT

I was dozing on the sofa, lazy as a Yule log, when the oldest boy
shook my shoulder and said, Let's go sleigh-riding on the NEW
hill. As if the hill had popped up overnight.

Look, I said, don't shake me like that when I am lying here
thinking of how to feed this family for the coming week.

Oh, be a sport, said my wife.

The new hill, it turned out, was a series of hills barreling over
one another down toward the river, like a school of happy porpoises.
Way over there, where the hills took a last drop, there was a general jubilation of voices, such as you hear around a crowded swimming pool in the summer time, and toward that sound dozens of
people were plodding ant-like across the white table-top of snow.
The snow crunched underfoot like stale cake icing. Just right,
said the oldest.

Up the flank of a nearby slope was a row of V-marks left by
a pair of climbing skis, fossil backbone of a giant catfish.

How I WISH I had some skis, I said to the boys, praising the
angels I hadn't.

(Once in a local sports shop I put on a pair, and, just standing
there, fell over into the tricycles.)

We came to the brink of the last hill and looked down. I
wished I'd stayed with the tricycles. There was, I estimated, a 65
degree incline for about 50 feet and then it really got down to
business and steepened into 85 degrees.

Or maybe 90.

Hill nothing.

It was a cliff.

A country mile high.

Boys, boys, I said, Guybo has left something in the car.

The oldest was already off at a run, falling on the sled with a rattling ka-thump, snow spuming from the runners, then zipping over the brink and out of sight, until he reappeared on the meadow far below, a ground-skimming swallow.

Back up the hill he offered the sled to his brother who shook his head.

I don't know how to get on it, he said, big-eyed.

Guybo will show you, I said. (Keep this sled moving up and down the hill, and keep off it, I thought.)

See, I said, you just lie down, grab the steering bar like this, firmly and—HEY, WHO'S PUSHING ME!

EVERYBODY was pushing, and the sled was gliding down the first slope, and then jumping forward abruptly as if it meant to take off.

By George, I thought, as we hurtled over the fold of the first incline, By George, I've shot right off the sled and am soaring along like a bird. Shall I spread my arms and try to glide to a landing or ball up like a doodle-bug and roll in?

But no, I felt beneath me, and the sled was still there, two or three inches below me, but still there, if we should ever decide to touch earth again.

Then the sled was bouncing through choppy white shingles, a spinning white kaleidoscope three inches from my nose.

Just ahead was the river.

Roll off this thing, I told myself, and let it go in the drink alone. There are sleds and sleds but only one Guybo.

I made a beautiful turtle-like turn off the sled, and, marveling at my own grace under such pressure, forgot to let go of the sled, and there it was RIDING ME for perhaps 10 yards. We stopped at the bank, amid cheers of persons who had been watching, open-mouthed, the mad, mad ride.

The boys fell all over me when I got back to the top.

Showboat, said my wife.

# WATERMELON, FOR REMEMBRANCE

Watermelons were strewn along the sidewalk, seal-like. When I stooped to thump them with my finger, the 5-year-old wanted to know why.

It's part of buying a watermelon, I told him, like you kick the tires of an automobile and nod your head wisely when the engine is ready to fall out. To be honest, one melon sounds like another to me. I guess you thump on a watermelon like you knock on wood.

The only true test is when you take the melon home. It has been that way since childhood when you bought the melon—a fat, dark green monster—off the back of a wagon for a quarter and wrestled it up on top of the linoleum table in the kitchen.

Your father took the butcher knife—the blade almost worn in two—and, while you capered about barefooted and the dog barked, he cut the melon, the knife sliding around the dark green sides, a little streak of red glow running just ahead of the blade and the melon cracking open, a sudden flaring of red pitted with jet black seeds. As a moment of truth, it matched the time when you opened the top of the freezer and pulled out the wooden dash all clumped with ice cream.

The watermelon is the Old King Cole of fruits, a jolly super-abundant clown. It cheers you to look at him. It demands to be eaten. There are those who eat it plain, and those who eat it with salt, and those who eat the melon half-way plain and finish off with salt. I always begin by meaning to use salt and end by never touching the shaker.

Some of my friends don't care for watermelon. Others can take it or leave it, although how they can be so coolly objective about something as emphatic as a watermelon is beyond me.

There's nothing as democratic as a watermelon feast. A person just can't be finicky and high toned eating watermelon. It just reaches out and grabs you. Those Flemish painters of great gatherings of people, the Brueghel brothers, should have done a church watermelon picnic, the long bare planks, the knives, forks, and salt cellars, and folks eating happily, most of them with a faint red wash of melon juice around their mouths.

It's a child's fruit. You can dig trenches in it, and lakes, and dikes, and see how close you can eat to the green, and then, when it's finished, cut teeth out of the rind for funny faces.

I bought the melon and was wrestling it in the house, while the boy capered about and the dog barked, when, going up the back steps, I slipped and the melon fell. My wife heard the explosion and came to survey the wreckage.

What a memory this child is going to have, she said.

---

# THE TRAP THAT THOUGHT BIG

Stop the car! called my wife. Save that poor bird!

I stepped on the gas.

From the tone of her voice I guessed that the bird was in the clutches of (a) a larger bird, an eagle maybe, or (b) a grizzly bear, the first ever seen at Cole's Point.

Roll up the windows, everybody, I shouted, and keep calm.

It turned out that the bird, flapping around like a ragged black scarf, was caught in a crab trap left on the river bank.

It was the first such trap I'd ever seen, a wire cage divided into little compartments that opened one into another until finally the crab found himself in the last back hall without enough sense to back out. A bit of shell had drawn the bird into the cage.

I thought birds had more sense, I said.

Hurry, said my wife. Free the poor thing.

Listen, I said, let's think this thing through. This trap has already caught a crab and a bird. I don't like the way it's going up the scale.

You're afraid, she cried. Afraid of that little bird!

AFRAID MY EYE! I shouted. What is there to be afraid of? Not a day goes by but what I don't stick my hand into a cage with a bird that has a beak the size of a medicine dropper.

I picked up the trap with my left hand and extended my right in and out of the little compartments, as if crocheting a sleeve, all the way to the shoulder. The bird squawked something awful. Over our heads his fellow formed a funnel, cawing and cussing. Bite 'im, bite 'im, it sounded like they were saying.

Oh, I see how it's done, said my wife, grabbing the bottom side of the cage. All you do is yank this away and—

The bird flew out and was soon a black beebee in the distance, and then nothing.

I started to pull out my arm and the jagged wire ends in the doorways jabbed me to a stop.

By George, I said, I'm trapped.

For 15 minutes we struggled with the trap. Then, while I crouched in the back seat, we drove to the crossroads store up the way. Three fellows sat out front on soft drink crates, waiting for something to happen.

Now, look, I said softly to the 7-year-old, the middle boy with the face as bland as country butter. Now look, when you go in there and ask for pliers, don't try to tell some preposterous story that nobody would swallow. Keep it simple and keep it believable.

He bounced out of the car and went into the dark cavern of the store, and presently, in the Summer stillness, above the July flies, we could hear him asking:

Please, sir, may I borrow some pliers to get my fa-ther out of a crab trap?

---

## SUMMER ROMANCE

Just call it a Summer romance between a dog and a family.

No one saw the dog approach the first time.

He was simply in our midst on the beach, his tail wagging in dignified greeting, his broad face almost beaming, it seemed, at having found us.

Well, you finally got here, he seemed to say.

He was fairly heavy, more than 60 pounds, the oldest boy said, trying to lift him. He was built close to the ground on bowed, stocky legs which led one child to remark, as the dog came trundling forward, that he looked like an elephant walking. In coloring, he was almost cow-like, most of him white except for a pair of big, lapping, brown ears and a brown splash or two on his sides.

He was part beagle hound, and that accounted for his curiosity that made him a sturdy beachcomber, and he was part basset hound, and that explained the air of quiet ennui with which he observed, with sad, sloe eyes, the scene he investigated.

Two of us were sprawled on the beach playing checkers, the board between us, when the dog ambled over and sat down to watch the game. His braced front feet slipped lower and lower into the sand, as if the effort of watching were almost too much for him, and then, suddenly, he leaned forward, and with his broad nose gently shoved a checker from one square to the other. In the laughter my wife exclaimed that he looked like one of the dogs drawn by Thurber. The name stuck, and the children insisted that he knew it.

Nothing upset his sense of heavy dignity, not even when the children sat him in a bushel basket atop a sand heap for the first shot at the moon.

When he dug in the beach on his short legs, it was in a churning slow motion that didn't carry the sand from under his low-slung body. Sometimes he would lie on his side and dig abstractedly with one paw. He would wade belly deep into the brackish river and lap fastidously at the salt water, then wade ashore.

He'd watch with stolid interest from the sidelines when the children started a project on the beach, and then, his beagle curiosity overcoming his basset reserve, he would mosey into the midst of the action. Seeing them at work on a spreading, elaborate sand castle, he walked forward, dug out one side, and flopped down with a heavy sigh. They buried him in sand to the collar line, and he took it quietly.

When the adults shook out the light, bright spread, it ballooned like a tent top in the breeze, and at just the precise moment that it sank gently to the ground, Thurber would stalk to the center and sit down, dignified as a white chalk statue of a dog on a beach

For long moments he would regard an adult reading or playing cards, and then, politely, irresistibly, he would move his big head forward and give his human friend a sloppy lick on the ear.

How much a part of the picture he had become . . . or maybe it should be the other way around. . . . . How much a part of the picture WE had become on his beach, I didn't realize until we started home. There were no tears, just a mutinous poking out of under lips when I said the dog had to stay.

He's not even our dog, I said, illogically.

That was why, what money I had left clutched in my hand, I went up and down the beach in the dark knocking at doors, asking about a big little dog, with brown ears, holding my hand about this high off the ground.

Nobody knows where that brown-eared beagle lives, said one man. He just shows up every morning.

I know the dog you're talking about, said another—that white basset hound, but I don't know his owner. Isn't he the one ugliest dog you ever saw?

Look at it this way, I said to a silent car as we bumped off toward the highway, Look at it this way. Thurber was the supervisor of that beach, the presiding spirit, the host. He has a job to do. He wouldn't have been happy away from the beach, and he'll be here to welcome us next year.

More cold silence.

Look, I shouted, I'll find a dog EXACTLY like Thurber. They're a dime a dozen.

Do you promise? asked the middle boy, the one who holds me to what I say.

I promise! Now forget Thurber, will ya? He's happy where he is.

But I'm not.

Anybody know where I can get a dog, part basset, part beagle?

---

## WINTER RENDEZVOUS

NO POWER ON EARTH CAN MOVE ME TO GET A DOG, I said, Christmas eve or not.

Of course not, said my wife.

Listen, I said. Let me tell you about dogs. They track up the house, they turn over garbage cans, and they break your heart.

You should know, she said.

Why? I asked, suspiciously.

You were never without one as a boy.

Things are different.

You're older, she said.

I'm going to call the dog man and tell him that UNDER NO CIRCUMSTANCES do I want the dog.

That's hardly necessary, she said. It's been more than four months since he offered it.

(Right after a vacation column about a dog on the beach —part-bassett, part-beagle—that alienated my family's affections.)

I went to the phone, chatted a moment, came back, and started putting on my coat. My wife said, Where are you going?

I'm going over to his house on the other side of town and TELL HIM TO HIS FACE that I don't want the dog, I said.

I don't blame you, said my wife. There's so little to do on Christmas Eve.

The man took me in his flood-lit backyard and whistled and out from under the house ran four short-legged beagle bassets, whimpering in excitement, dappled white and brown that varied from light caramel to a deep chocolate, like a swirling butterscotch sundae under foot. I put down my hand and it was like patting a super-soft moving rug.

I'll take all four, I said.

With some difficulty my friend held me to taking only one, and as I left, he called: It's been four months, but I knew you'd get here.

Opening the door at home, I tossed the dog to the floor, and he bounded, like a skipping stone, into my wife's arms.

I hope you're satisfied, I said. I wash my hands of that dog.

But he was one of the gentlest, most well-mannered puppies it's been my privilege to meet. He didn't make a sound all night, as long as I lay beside him on the floor.

Early in the morning when the boys were stirring, I whisked the dog into the living room, under the lighted tree, where he pattered in an excited soft-shoe dance on the rug until the door opened and the three of them shot into the flickering red, blue and green gloom. Two of them headed straight for their gifts, but the third, the 7-year-old caught sight of the dog, and flapping his arms like a rooster that's lost its voice, took fully 10 secounds before he was able to shout: A LIVE DOG!

# AUTOMATION, TAKE IT AWAY

Edward Teller noted in a speech the other day that one day machines will have the capacity to make decisions.

Mr. Teller, they have ALREADY begun working on the less intelligent among us. You hear persons say that someone can't get along with people. I can't even get along with THINGS. They are out to trap me.

I never met a machine I didn't dislike.

Just the other week I was in a conference with some pret-ty big people, let me tell you, and had just about swung them to my view, so I began shaking hands all around and even heard one of the big shots say to the other: You know, Friddell's not near the jerk I thought he was.

I was turning to go, glowing with bonhomie, when the long spiraled cord on the desk telephone snaked out ACROSS THE FLOOR, grabbed my ankle, and leveled me into a flying dive across the room so I belly-busted flat on the carpet, my chin in the nap. Well, of course, such an attempted exit ended serious consideration of ANY subject. The deal fell through right there. I was just glad the rug was soft. Be grateful for small favors, is my motto, and get up and try again.

Somebody wrote a book called "The Tyranny of Things," meaning, I guess, don't dedicate yourself to getting material things. With me there's a different emphasis: Don't let the things get YOU, like the goblins got Orphan Annie. It's a much more active tyranny than the book ever realized.

In my first job the boss had a big paneled office in which there were two identical doors about a yard apart. One opened into the corridor. The other opened into a closet. Turning to leave and seeing them side by side, I was never sure which door opened into what.

Walking across the room toward the two doors, feeling the boss's somewhat satiric eyes on my back, I'd be debating inwardly, Now is it the right that gets you out of here or does that open

into that plaguey closet?  It was "The Lady or the Tiger?" all
over again.

I had reason to worry.  The first time he summoned me to
his office I didn't notice the door contretemps, and, on the way
out, glancing back as I turned the knob to toss him a gay, parting
bon mot, I plunged directly into the clothes closet, banged the door
behind me, and fell to threshing around in coat-hangers and umbrellas.

Are you all right in there, Friddell?

Quite.

Can I help you?

No trouble.  Just looking for my coat.

You were wearing it when you went in.

By George, so I was, or am, or . . . How do I get out of here?

Don't tell me anything about machines, Mr. Teller.  I've been
fighting on that front for a LONG ole time.

---

# ADVENTURES IN OLD - TIME STORES

One day Ike's golf game was rained out, and he spent a Saturday poking around an old-time country store.  For Mamie, he said.
He found an old-time coffee grinder, dark red, like the one, he
said, that he used to crank "by the hour" as a grocery clerk.

What I remember best about the old-time store is that THINGS
HAPPENED.

In today's supermarket, everything is mechanized.  Has to be.
Even the customers.

You pace up and down the aisles, leaning on a rubber-tired cart,
reaching to the right and the left, in a sort of trance until the basket
is full, and then, robot-like, push the cart to the check-out counter,
dreamily empty your pockets, and wander out through a door that
swings open by itself with just a suggestion of a hiss.

I have yet to see a butcher in a modern supermarket.  There's
just a hand reaching out now and then from a sliding panel, as in
"The Cat and the Canary" in our senior class play, grabbing up a

pound of ground round and disappearing behind the panel.

Spooky.

There's a little button over the long white porcelain meat trough. RING FOR SERVICE, it says.

Catch me pushing that bell? Ha! YOU push it. Not Guybo. The robots might get me.

My wife told me that if you peer through the dark glass sliding down the back of the meat case, you could see the butchers moving around, darkly, in the no-man's land behind the trick mirror.

Like looking, she said, through fathoms of water at the sea bottom.

You look, I told her. I'll stay out here in the bright lights. I'd just as soon not know about such things, I added. Life's complicated enough.

In fact, I may become a vegetarian.

Or let her buy the roast.

Back in the old days you SAW the butcher, a jolly red-faced fellow with slicked-down blue-black hair. You could see back where he worked, too, in his store within a store, arranged as neatly as a girl's play house marked out on the ground, the big chopping block in the center, the clean sawdust on the floor.

He stood right there in plain view, heavy-set as one of his beeves, dealing out his wares with his big sausage-mottled arms. He didn't pop in and out from behind sliding mirrors, leaving a disconcerting impression of a hand, an eyebrow, an ear, abstract bits of a jigsaw puzzle.

He hardly ever said a word, just smiled, winked, and shook silently with laughter at what went on in the store.

There was the dog-food salesman, a stringy, fast-talking fellow, who offered to eat his own product to prove its purity. The butcher, without saying a word, broke open a box of crackers, and the salesman spread on the dogfood carefully, as if he were preparing a culture for the discovery of penicillin. Before an audience of clerks, housewives, and dogs, he popped three helpings in his mouth, smacking his lips, saying, Hm-m-m hm!

Then the dogfood salesman keeled over in a faint.

It was those dern crackers, he said later.

# MUSINGS OF A MILQUETOAST

You'd never guess that beneath this dashing, gay exterior is a craven soul. I make Casper Milquetoast look like the Siegfried Line.

You're familiar, I know, with the sort of fellow who, when he sits down beside you in the packed, general admission stands, says, after a few seconds, HEY, SAVE THIS SEAT WILL YA? and goes rollicking off.

I can no more say No to him than I can say Yes to the bluff party who comes along 15 seconds later and says, settling down like the Graf Zeppelin, IS THIS SEAT TAKEN, BUD?

All I can do is wait and hope that when the first party returns and sees the second party in his seat, the two will fight each other, and not me.

Usually , the first party returns and stands in the aisle, hands on hips, staring at the place where his seat used to be, such an expression of astonishment on his face it's almost worth the embarrassment to see it.

I commence to shrug my shoulders and wigwag my hands, indicating that the whole situation has got so complicated it would be impossible to explain without endangering our relations along the Caspian seacoast, and off he stomps in disbelief.

But that embarrassment is nothing to opening your front door onto a roomful of your wife's bridge club.

For a second there's a dense thicket of noise, as of a great flock of birds getting set to fly, and then, abruptly, silence.

And stares.

Even your wife looks faintly unfamiliar.

It's over in a flash, but it's a moment to remember—and avoid another time.

## SPRING RINGS

They don't play marbles like they useta, said the oldest man on the newspaper's copy desk.

You mean they play with square marbles now, said the cub on the horseshoe's rim.

I mean they don't play as often, said the oldest. Another thing, you didn't have to encourage kids to play marbles. They did it like frogs croak in the spring. These days they get special courts and supervision and trips to Bermuda, but I don't see any kids playing marbles. It used to be, when Spring came, the world was just one big marble, criss-crossed with rings that held a million more marbles. I wore out corduroy knickers so fast my mother sewed on leather knee pads. I wore right through those, too. You can see the callous on my shooting knuckle yet, said the oldest man and passed his hand around for all to see.

You must have been a champion, said the youngest.

In a way, he admitted, I was. It began, he said, when my father gave me six red agates on my seventh birthday. I felt something hard under my pillow that morning, pulled out a soft leather pouch, and out rolled the agates. They were of varying sizes, like the eggs my mother used to find in the hens she cut open for Sunday dinner. There's another thing, said the oldest man, women don't seem to skin chickens any more.

Get on with the six red agates, said the cub.

Well, he said, they ranged from English pea size to one larger than the end of my thump and they were a deep milk red with a hint of buried suns. They made a nice soft thud when they hit another marble, and for days I didn't take them out of my pocket around the older boys.

One day I did take out the agates, maybe to impress the oldest boy in the neighborhood, a 12-year-old named Oscar who pomaded his hair into a slick black cap. In a matter of minutes Oscar had me in a game and when he had picked up all the agates, I found we'd been playing for keeps. I went home, biting my lower lip to keep from crying, and found my father getting ready to paint the house while my mother was away visiting her sister for two weeks.

My father was a happy-go-lucky man, but my mother had said he should not paint our rambling old house by himself, and so he was going to special pains to do it, even to buying white painter's overalls in which he was dressed when I moped up biting my lip. He had paint cans spread all over our latticed back porch where we lived all Spring and Summer, and he was mixing paint a mile a minute.

You know, said the oldest man, I hadn't thought of it, but you don't see latticed back porches any more. The whole world lives on a stoop.

The agates, said his junior.

My father was a seismograph when it came to other people's feelings, and happy as he was mixing paint he could feel the cloud on the horizon which was me. In no time he had picked me clean as a hickory nut. First he started out after Oscar, then he started to send me by myself, and finally he said, wait a minute, we've got to think this thing through and sat down on a paint can, the only unopened one on the whole back porch.

Let's go, he said, I've got it, and leaving the opened cans, we rushed off in the Jewett to the Woco-Pep station where my father picked out a handful of steelies, little and big ball bearings. We went to my grandmother's on the other side of town. Without so much as a hello to her, he got a broom off the back porch and swept away the green-gold oak tassles that powdered the ground, drew a deep black circle in the dirt, and we began playing marbles.

My grandmother looked out the kitchen window presently, and there was a great deal of conversation that could be heard in the next block about some men who never grew up, and the cook, who had known my father almost as long as my grandmother had, said Lawd yes.

My father said to me in a low voice, Never stop to explain anything to people who won't understand anyway and most of all women, and we went on playing marbles.

At the end of two weeks I had developed what you would call a soft touch with a wicked little steelie.

Now pretend I am Oscar, said my father, and let's see how you shoot, only when your turn comes with the real Oscar, think of him as nobody.

So I would think of my father as Oscar and plug the marbles all the way up in the roots of the oak tree. My father handed me six more agates, swatted me on the back and said, If you lose, don't feel too bad too long, but I don't think you'll lose.

Off I went and found Oscar and tossed my six new agates back and forth in the air like beautiful suns.

Let's play, he said.

For keeps? I asked.

For keeps.

All right, I said, if I shoot first.

Shoot, he said, and threw down my six old agates.

He never got a shot. My little silver steelie spun like a top around the ring, knocking agates hither and yon. By sundown my pockets hung like gourds with marbles. All but the agates I divided among the boys who had been losing all week to Oscar.

My father smiled when I came home with the lustrous handful of agates. They made a soft clatter as he rattled them in his fist.

You won, he said, but even had you lost, you made an honest effort and that counts the most. Only remember, the world is full of Oscars and on any given day he might be you or me or anybody.

What did you do with the paint, I asked.

Threw it in the ditch, he said, it was of very poor quality.

When my mother came home from my aunt's she told my father she was glad he hadn't tried anything so foolish as painting this big barn of a house. But later, fixing supper, she told me she was afraid my father was getting old. She could have sworn when she left he was going to paint the house.

I pulled the dozen agates out of my pocket and said, Maybe he didn't have the money after buying me six more agates.

My mother studied me a minute, but I didn't crack a smile.

I swear, she said, you're getting more like him every day.

She couldn't have pleased me more.

It's a beautiful story, said the cub on the copy desk, and I wish you could prove it.

My father's dead, said the oldest man, and Oscar's in Chicago, but I still have this.

The oldest man opened his hand and in the lined brown palm lay a deep red agate with just the hint of a sun in its milky depths.

# THE BRAVE CIRCUS

Round up the boys, I shouted, banging in the back door.
There's an elephant in town!

Has he broken loose? cried my wife.

Not yet I said, but if he does, we want to be there to see
EVERY MINUTE OF IT.

There is but one abiding rule in my life, I told her: If an
elephant comes within 15 miles of you, GO LOOK AT IT. It may
be the last elephant you'll see.

In the end we went to see the elephant which was lending his
royal presence to a circus. It desperately needed the elephant.
It could not hold the hat of the circus playing in Madison Square
Garden. Raw bones peeped through its gaudy rags. First you
were aghast, then entranced at its poverty. Like watching a bull-
fighter without a sword or a cape. Just him, bare-handed, and
ze bool. Whole MINUTES of truth.

In Madison Square Garden, the acts are smothered in plumes
and spangles.

Glittering lies.

Out on the State Fair Grounds, with the cruel sun stabbing
through the sieve-like tent top, everything was out in the open.
Embarrassingly so.

In the great Ringling cirus, the aerial artists flit about in the
wires of the big top unreal as butterflies. How much more suspense
in seeing an AMATEUR trapeze troupe, almost as if your own
family were up there. Without a net.

And the dog act.

Not spitzes or Samoyedes, no canine Einsteins, bred for the
ring, just ordinary dogs that might have been whistled out of the
alley. Pets.

At the most, I figured, there were two families, frantically
changing costumes out back, bolting in and out of the big top. That
circus was the saddest— and bravest—I ever saw, reduced to
nothing BUT showmanship.

The flourish of the hand, right down to the last flip of the fingertips to acknowledge, gracefully, the applause that wasn't there.

After the show we went back for a last look at the elephant, dust-covered, with great dark patches of wet about its eyes, like a sad-faced clown, nodding his big head, as full of boulders and hollows as a contour map of a bare mountain, the pendulum snout swinging, snake-like, back and forth.

There was a motion in front of the great nodding head. I looked down. My 6-year-old, his face solemn, was bent over, holding his ankle with one hand, the other arm swinging before him like a snout, a spontaneous tribute to his majesty, the elephant.

There's nothing like an elephant.

There's nothing like a circus.

However poor.

# REFLECTIONS OF A POTATO-HEAD

My wife was down town the other day, waiting for the light to change, when she saw me barging along the opposite side of the street and heard one fellow say to another: Look over there at old Potato-Head.

I have what the barbers call a "problem head."

It starts off on a normal course, tapers just a little, deceptively, as if going down, but then bulges out, drops, and cuts back sharply in a Great Overhang, as the barbers say.

The new barber starts clipping away at the front, whistling tunelessly, as if all were well, works along toward the center, humming "The Barcarolle" from Verdi, when suddenly he is no longer singing, but is panting hoarsely, a mountain climber who finds himself slipping and sliding on a steep slope he didn't even know existed.

The other day, as I was taking my seat before a new barber, a veteran five chairs down yelled: WATCH THAT OVER-HANG, CLIFF!

No amount of caution helps. The barber finds himself dangling on that precipice, clipping wildly for a foothold. On top again, he has to take off a little more up there for conformity, to blend with the big boulder on the back slope, and then, working back carefully, he takes one slip too many, and is over the edge again, screaming with his scissors for a foothold.

Often, a barber—in business for 20 or 30 years—will stop in the middle of the job and go stare out in the street, wordlessly.

All this builds up a sort of tension in me too. I put off going for a haircut, five weeks this trip, and my friends begin saying, Get a violin! or put on a collar! and other things so brilliant that I cannot even put them down on paper for laughing so hard.

The haircut done, there's more merriment from the bleachers, remarks like potato-head from passersby. Last night, going to a party in Bon Air, my wife said, Now try to show the back of your head as little as possible.

I went around most of the evening my hand clasped to the back of my head, as if in deep thought or tried to stand with my back to the wall, making only an occasional dash to the center of the room to spear a pineapple chunk from a fruit compote. I was like some shy, woodland bird, the ugly-headed vireo.

Bidding the guests good-by, I backed around the room, smiling politely, murmuring nothings, bowing just a little here and there, so that as we escaped into the blessed darkness, someone in the company asked in bewilderment: WHO was THAT? Mr. Moto?

---

# HOW TO DECORATE A TREE

It's strange that a thing as simple as a Christmas tree should present so many points of difference.

Most women, including my wife, prefer what they call a small, sensible, well-behaved tree, the kind that does not shed needles on the rug and knows its place.

My vote is for the sprawling, lurching variety, the kind that springs open-armed, balsam-eyed on company, as if it's glad to see them. A great, shaggy, uncouth tree. It would as lief fall on you as not.

Shopping unchaperoned, I would get a tree that would fill a whole front room. Guests would have to hack their way in with hatchets and drop a trail of bright pebbles to find their way out.

Occasionally, we would send expeditions for parties lost, caroling, in its dark green depths.

What I want is a TREE, the kind you yell TIMBER for when you see it falling slowly toward the sideboard, not a SHRUB.

But the debate over size and kind is as nothing compared to the question of when to put it up.

Right away, I say.

Tomorrow, on the first morning in December, the maddening urge to deck the tree begins to grow. I will scan every street corner eagerly for the first tree man, blowing his fingers, stamping his feet in the cold.

See, I'll say, SEE, it's time to put up the Christmas tree.

Putting up the tree is the one chore on earth that does not seem like work.

There's all the hipping and hopping about concerned with hauling out the decorations, dropping and smashing ornaments that have been in the family 300 years, and arguing over how to put on the icicles. (She places them singly, daintily, precisely as the drops on a chandelier. I back off 12 feet and fire away, blizzard-like.)

In her mind Santa should put up and decorate the tree late Christmas Eve.

When the old boy is staggering from assembling a tin garage set, or from racing round town to all-night drug stores looking for last-minute gifts. These wild forays on drug stores have produced some memorable gifts. Anyway, the recipients won't forget them, ever. I wish you could have seem my father-in-law's face when he opened my present to him and saw that perfectly gorgeous shower curtain.

My wife believes the late rush is worth the awe in the eyes of the young ones when they see, for the first time, the galaxy of blue, green, and red light shining in the darkened room, as if the magical old elf had only that moment slipped out the front door.

Last year we did a good deal of re-decorating AFTER Christmas when the stores cut prices by half on ornaments. I added three strings of lights, and we were all standing around admiring my economy, when, one by one, the lights began to blink out.

NO WONDER THEY SOLD THESE LIGHTS DIRT CHEAP, I shouted. THEY'RE ALL GOING OUT.

Then they began to blink on again.

These are blinker lights, explained my wife. They go on and off constantly.

One of the young ones pointed overhead. In the darkened room, the blinking, colored lights were casting exotic patterns on the ceiling, spires, stars, globes, in quick succession.

As if, he said, some one were painting, fast.

It really makes no difference when you put up a Christmas tree.

---

# WITHOUT A SPONSOR, YET

I hope the younger generations watching TV don't get the mistaken notion that a fight in life is as exciting as one on the 21-inch screen.

The few fights I've seen in the round have ended quickly—with one punch—or dragged on intolerably with two guys circling each other, breathing and talking heavily until finally they got tired or dizzy and gave up and went home.

Try putting THAT on TV.

I have yet to see on TV one fighter draw a line in the dust with his toe, as we used to do, and say, I dare you to step over, and the other reply, I double-dare you, and the first one come back fast, I TRIPLE-dare you, and the second one say, smart-like: I am rubber, you are glue, bounce offen me and stick on you.

Then the first one says, fast-like, Ole dead buzzard lying on the hill, I one-it, and the second says, I two-it, because he's got to say it under the rules of the game, and they go on that way, turn by turn, down the line, until somebody says, I eight-it, and that ends the fight, and everybody goes home satisfied.

Generally, the weaker the story on TV, the longer the fight. There's a pattern. The bad guy hits the hero from behind his back with a piano. The hero rallies, but the villain gets him down, and, suddenly, the hero, flat on his back, summons a reserve of strength from somewhere and comes up with a straight right that dumps the villain all the way across the room into a bar, a horse trough, a china cabinet, or anything that can make a good smash.

Then the hero gets up, pulls the back of his hand across his mouth, brushes his hat, goes over to the bar for a quick pick-me-up.

There's another distortion, the amount of time spent consuming whisky. I don't see how Matt Dillon stays on his feet from week to week.

Why, in the westerns we used to see— we saw ONE a week, if we were lucky, on Saturday, and it cost a whole dime—the white-hatted hero (he never lost his hat, even in a fight) wouldn't even LOOK at strong drink. Neither would the villain. It was called fire-water and sold only to Indians to make them go on the warpath. Now whisky fills the gaps between the fights. It may be that way with some in real life, but not many could bear the strain.

Anyway, real life is much more challenging in continuing tensions. The TV hero goes riding off into a chanting sunset—and into another pat pattern for next week. Real life never throws you the same combination of circumstances. It may not look as exciting as a saloon brawl on television, but it's a good deal more demanding over the long haul. I don't see how we do it, sometimes.

And without a sponsor.

# PUT A HOTEL ON BOARDWALK

Everywhere people are playing Monopoly, moving me to remember when it swept the cauntry during the depression.

My best friend, Henry, got a Monopoly board for his birthday, but we didn't take much to it, until his father, looking over our shoulders, became interested in all that trading of property and paying of money back and forth.

Henry's father was a big, broad-shouldered businessman, with a bald head, maybe from beating it against the wall as most businessmen were doing then.

When we unfolded the board and began to count our money on the floor, Henry's father stopped pacing and bent down to watch. Pretty soon he was down there with us, and when his wife said, Come to supper, everybody, he said, Nonsense, Cora, put the food in the oven.

This astonished us. When we were playing baseball and Henry

heard his father's whistle for supper, he would stop whatever he was doing and run in the direction of the whistle. Once, in a tie game, he banged the ball into the creek at the end of the pasture and was just rounding second base when he heard his father's whistle, and, without breaking stride, ran right on out through centerfield and home.

To his house, I mean, not home plate.

Henry's father also extended his bed-time a trifle.

From 8 o'clock until midnight.

Night after night we played. About 7 o'clock the phone would ring at my house, and Henry's father would say, All set, Monop?

Be right over soon as I've done my homework, I'd say.

O pshaw, he'd say. Bring it over here. You can work faster with Henry.

Henry and I sat on the sofa doing our homework and his father would stride around like a lion before feeding time, throwing us hints, bigger and bigger clues, until finally he was throwing us the answers.

Whew! he would say, when we were done. Glad THAT'S over. Cora, can't you speak to the teacher about giving these boys so much homework?

Then we would settle down to the real business of the evening, Monopoly. Henry's mother, just about perfect as a mother, and his sister, likewise, didn't give a fig for trading property, and they were happy to go broke as soon as possible and leave.

To be honest, neither Henry or I ever played unless his father was present. The sight of his big, genial father, slightly hunched over the board, his bald head gleaming in the lamp light, hiding his property cards carefully, bargaining for a half hour to get a card he wanted, slowly, reluctantly counting out money when he hit one of your hotels—the sight of him taking the game so intensely, made it exciting for everyone involved.

For the first of many occasions, big and little, I realized that one way to enjoy life is to engage in it strenuously.

It's been 20 years since I've seen Henry or his father, but I hear, indirectly, they have fared well in business. One pay day, when I'm feeling flush I shall put in a long distance call to my old home town, and when Henry's father answers the phone, I shall ask: All set, Monop?

## SHOOT - OUT AT SUNDOWN

Now whatever you do, said my wife as I rang the doorbell, don't get into any argument at this party. The talk in there is light and happy.

It was, too. The chatter from inside sounded as light as glass Chinese chimes, gay as "Nola" on the xylophone.

Listen, I said, the last thing I want to do is get into an argument, but I am just like Billy the Kid. They won't let me alone. Everytime I go into a crowded room, I hear the theme music from "High Noon."

Don't be childish, she said.

That's what they kept saying to Billy, too, I told her.

Just then the door opened, and, amid gay cries of the two women, the hostess said, exulting: "Would you believe it? There hasn't been one word of politics all evening!"

But as we entered the room, somewhere from its dim reaches, over near the hors d'oeuvres, came a glad bellow: "There's old Friddell. He believes in foreign aid."

I sighed. Here it was again. The challenge. It would have been the same had he said there's ole Friddell who DOESN'T believe in foreign aid.

I'll pick up the dare no matter how it's put, argue one way by the bric-a-brac and just the opposite across the room by the hi-fi, so that in one gathering two fellows fell to arguing over how I was arguing.

In a moment we were in the thick of it on foreign aid. More and more were drawn into the vortex of the debate until suddenly I was on the outskirts yelling my opinions to nobody in particular and realized that I could drift into the dining room to the shrimp bowl where a mild-mannered fellow ventured an observation on the race for Governor.

I replied, just as mildly, but I might as well have yelled. "They're off!" because in a second, it was as if eight of us were in a hard-fought Kentucky Derby. Out of the corner of my eye I saw that my adversary on foreign aid had come up and joined my side of the argument, so I shifted over to the viewpoint of the mild-mannered fellow who was out-gunned anyway.

Things got so brisk that I gave up the shrimp as a lost cause and ranged on into the kitchen where, getting a glass of water, I made a reasonable remark on federal aid to education, more to a water faucet than anybody else, but it was as if I had stumbled over a switch at Cape Canaveral. The whole kitchen went into orbit.

Later, as we were departing down the walk, my wife said, I hope you're satisfied. Just listen to that noise now.

There was nothing Nola about it. No Chinese wind chimes. It was more as if a bowling alley had gone berserk.

I'm not only satisfied, I said. I'm elated. It was a GRET party.

---

# BED-CHECK CHARLEY FLIES AGAIN

My Army outfit was the most wonderful ever formed. It filled everybody that saw it with wonder.

It was put together in 1942 when the draft board was scraping the bottom of the barrel. For us it turned the barrel inside out. Realizing its mistake, the Army tried to ship half the outfit back into civilian life, but the men bawled like civilians being drafted. The Army gave up

Near the end, waiting to go home, we used to have to wake up nearly every night and run for the air-raid shelters because of a lone Zero that would fly over the area, so high that it almost seemed stationary, so regular that we called him "Bed-Check Charley."

I have always been a slow waker. By the time I woke up and got out, on the run, the others would just be hurrying back. Nearly every morning, on sick call, there were two or three who, as they put it, "Friddell ran into."

One Sunday, while I was away on an all-day swimming detail at the other end of the island, my four tent-mates decided, impulsively, to lower the tent floor by five feet and save running to the air-raid shelter.

Won't ole Friddell be surprised when he sees this? they crowed as they dug.

At about 10 o'clock that night they finished, doused the lights, fell on their canvas cots, and fell asleep. At 11 o'clock the truck returned with the swimming detail, and I hurried toward the tent through the starless night, thinking how lucky I was to have four such comrades, men of good will all, thinking how happy they would be when I sang out, Here's your ole buddy-buddy back safe and sound.

Hello, fellows, I shouted, stepping into the dark tent, Here's your ole buddy-buddy back — WHAMBAMMEDYBAMBAM-SLAM.                    ,

It seemed I would never stop falling . . . through the mosquito net rigging . . . through the canvas cot . . . through the foot-locker . . . almost through the ground. The explosive stages of my descent brought everybody off their cots in a sleep-fogged gallop, one of them bellowing, BED-CHECK CHARLEY'S GOT US!

WAKE FRIDDELL! another yelled as all four tore for the door, reeling back when they slammed against the walls, falling over each other in a shouting scramble.

FIND FRIDDELL, called one. WE'RE SINKING!

WAKE-UP, WAKE-UP FOR BED-CHECK CHARLEY, they yelled, making another run for the door that wasn't there. HE'S GOT US! LOOK OUT FOR BED-CHECK CHARLEY!

The guards heard and came hurtling through the night, bellowing to one and all, UP AND OUT FER BED-CHECK CHARLEY, UP AND OUT FER BED-CHECK CHARLEY!

One guard pinpointed the core of the commotion at our tent and came lunging through the door, calling, UPANDOUTFER——

As he floated through the air, astonished, his finger froze on the carbine trigger and shots whined and blasted through the tent tops to the right and left of us.

HE'S GOT ME! he bellowed as he landed. BED-CHECK'S GOT ME!

Men boiled out of tents all around us, seizing gas masks, machetes and cookies from home, and six more piled over the brink into our tent. After that, there was no more room to fall in. Order was restored, and we all went back to sleep, exhausted.

At about 1:30 a.m. Bed-Check Charley came over.

# THE FROSTED WHALE

We met the frosted whale on the midway.

As we staggered from the big top, still dazed, there came blaring down the midway:

COME AND SEE A REAL WHALE!

Families flew apart like peewees smacked with a steelie, and the children headed for the whale trailer.

Boys, boys, I shouted, come back and let Guybo tell you a secret.

What secret? asked my wife.

I'm broke.

Anyway, I said, that whale is obviously a—

SEE THE REAL WHALE! boomed the loudspeaker WEIGHS 16,000 POUNDS.

—fake, I finished.

How do you know? she asked.

How do I KNOW! They'll—

ARE WE GOING TO LET RUSSIA GET AHEAD OF US? boomed the speaker. LET YOUR CHILDREN SEE A REAL WHALE.

—never get me in there, I said.

In the barker's box was a grandmotherly lady holding a snake-head mike.

Up on a catwalk was a waddled, red-faced fellow who looked down into the trailer where we couldn't see and said, marveling, That tail is big enough to cut a boat in two.

EVERYBODY WANTS TO SEE THE WHALE WITH A MOUTHFUL OF HAIR, called the klaxon-voiced grandma.

I caught it myself, added the red-faced gent, on the catwalk.

HE'S KEPT IN FROST TO KEEP COOL, shouted the grandmother.

Look, I said to the oldest boy, here's a quarter. Go up and see what it's like.

The boy stood on the catwalk, the whaler's hand on his shoulder. The two looked down.

WHAT'S IT LIKE? I shouted, up to them.

The two talked earnestly.

I SAID WHAT'S IT LIKE?

No answer. I sent his two brothers. The three stood with the whaler, their heads together.

HELLO UP THERE, I bellowed. IS IT REAL?

OF COURSE IT IS, blared the grandma. DON'T MISS THE FROSTED WHALE.

I'm going up, said my wife.

So go up, I said, and kindly send me word what it's like by the next passing steamer.

She joined the symposium on whales. Excited by the sight of them, others crowded onto the catwalk.

I gave up.

I didn't want to make a spectacle of myself, shouting.

Especially when nobody would listen.

Driving home though, I asked, calmly, reasonably:

WHAT WAS IT LIKE?

Real except it had a flat look; sort of gray, only it wasn't; resting in water that was more like frost.

Like he was in the refrigerator, added the 6-year-old.

I wheeled the car around.

Where are you going? asked my wife, alarmed.

BACK TO SEE THE FROSTED WHALE, I shouted.

---

# 3 SODAS, 4 SPOONS

On a hot day like this, I told my wife, the only thing to do is get a chocolate ice cream soda, the way it used to be.

How did it used to be? she asked.

I don't remember EXACTLY, I said. I had no notion that the ice cream soda was going to vanish along with the buffalo and the whooping crane, or I'd have made notes.

But I do recall that the getting together of an ice cream soda wasn't a matter of seconds. It took MANY MINUTES. Whole hours, it seemed, on a hot day when heat waves rose off the tarred street and your shirt stuck to your back.

It was a careful building job.

First, the counter man put in a big shot of chocolate sauce and —get this—a large dollop of milk, REAL MILK, and stirred it briskly for a base. Then he added carbonated water, all foamy, and a hefty scoop of vanilla ice cream that brought the soda to the rim of the glass.

Next, while you watched anxiously to see whether there would be two or three dips, he ladled on a firm white cloud of whipped cream, honest whip cream, with body to it. He put a dash of chocolate chips on the puffy white mass, and topped it with a big red cherry.

He slid the glass down the marble counter toward you, seeing, if he were a smart aleck, how close he could slide it to the edge. Here came the big glass, belling out at the top, sliding along the black and white marble counter, almost at your eye level, a white streak or two already running down the brown side from the thick swirls of whipped cream topping, the glass beaded frostily.

Or maybe you were seated in a wire-backed chair at a little round marble-top table under a big four-bladed fan that churned the air as if IT were heavy whip cream. The counter man clunked the soda down before you with a heavy, satisfying THUNK. You took several seconds figuring how to go after that soda, it was so big. There were layers of flavors that stood out in stratas and then blended, and a stinging sensation in your nose from the carbonated water.

Did you always get chocolate? she asked.

ALWAYS, I said. It had to be chocolate.

Why don't you take the three boys to the drugstore and buy sodas for all four of you?

To tell you the truth, what one thing and another, I only have money for three sodas, and it would not be QUITE the same, watching THEM eat the sodas.

Nonsense, she said. You know the 5-year-old won't half finish his. That should be enough for you.

We went to the drugstore, and I ordererd three sodas.

What flavor? asked the counterman.

Chocolate, said the 9-year-old.

Chocolate, said the 7-year-old.

Strawberry, said the 5-year-old.

# MORAN, MACK, AND NOW THE MOON

What disconcerts me about the space age is that it's so all-fired sudden. I'm not accustomed to the pace.

I grew up in a time of small wonders, spaced comfortably apart. Nearly everything big had been discovered. Civilization was strolling along a pleasant plateau of endeavor. It was a plum, mellowing in the sun, brushed lightly by the wind of a passing butterfly.

New inventions, what few there were, were easy to soak up, arriving slowly. That business at Kitty Hawk was just a stunt, like flying a box kite. Radio was a tiny, static-filled toy. You could almost do as well with a waxed cord strung between two tin cans. All my uncles built crystal sets. (I can't even TURN ON the TV and get a clear picture.) They'd strap earphones on my head, and say, LISTEN, BOY, YOU'RE HEARING HISTORY!

All I got was Moran and Mack, sounding faint and far away, two crows in a pine tree. What made the biggest impact was the electric refrigerator. We got a new refrigerator, you'd say, and all would go in and try to figure whether the light went on or stayed off when you closed the door. Heavy stuff.

There was the advent of ice cubes. My grandfather wouldn't have 'em, swore they didn't get his tea as cold as chunk ice. I think he was right.

Then, in dizzying succession, we got dial telephones, popsickles and yo-yos.

Then, in a sort of break-through, we got TWO sticks in the popsickles and DOUBLE dip ice cream cones. The world had waited a long time for those advances.

My grandfather didn't like dial telephones, either. You lost the personal touch. I think he was right there too. There's nothing so infuriating as a busy signal.

Remember that old tune, "Hello, Central, Give Me Heaven?" How could you dial a message like that?

They won't last, my grandfather predicted.

I think he was right.

The yo-yo put us all in a spin. Walk the baby, around the world, over the moon . . .

These days they throw a yo-yo satellite AROUND the moon and back and take its picture.

Discoveries come so thick and fast you don't recover from one before another drops on you.

I was all braced for the next move in space when the United States put a submarine UNDER the North Pole.

The full force of this didn't come home to me until weeks later I bought a world globe on sale. (I may not understand what's up, but I'm determined the next generation shall. Somebody's got to save us.)

That night I was spinning the globe, watching the colors blend (yo-yo like) when suddenly I missed the North Pole.

Honey, I yelled, no wonder they sold this globe cheap. They left off the North Pole.

Look again, she advised.

There's no North Pole, I insisted. No big white glob on the globe. Just a confounded little metal tag with numbers on it.

That metal tag, she said, IS the North Pole. It's just an ice cap.

No, I pleaded. It's one of the seven continents. I've known it all my life. Meant to go there and explore after I'd finished the Orinoco. There are igloos. and Eskimo kids with slant eyes in round gingerbread faces who eat chocolate-covered ice cream pies in aluminum foil, and polar bears that look for the North Wind, and—

Yes, she said, and just the other month we sent a submarine under it.

I surrendered. Science had cut the ground right out from under my feet.

I'm afraid to look up the Orinoco.

It may be a super-highway.

# FIRST HAT — LAST, TOO

I said good-by to my youth the other day.

Bought a hat.

Doctor's orders. Flu and all.

By the way, he said, in his dry way, Buy a hat.

Tell me the AMA isn't powerful.

Numbly, I went to the store, and stood while the clerk placed one after another on my noggin.

The Anthony Eden homburg, he announced.

Happy Hooligan, I thought, gazing in the mirrow.

The high-crowned Main Street magnate, he intoned.

Hoot Gibson.

The dashing Swiss yodeler, he said, and even HE broke down at THAT.

(At the Hat Institute they tell them, Never NEVER, laugh at the customer. But this fellow cracked.)

He dug back in the stock and found a hat so conservative it must have been there since William Henry Harrison.

Walking out the door, I felt sedate, settled.

A respectable citizen instead of Sidney Carton (played by Ronald Colman) going to the guillotine.

Oh, 'tis a far better thing I do than I have ever done, 'tis a far better place to which I go than I have ever known.

I bet I could borrow money at the bank on this hat. Make a new start.

Thirty feet away Sam Moore was approaching and Sam's face got a strange, wary look, as if he saw an elephant blowing down the street and was deciding which way to duck. Then it cleared, and he shouted, Why it's YOU, and fell against a parking meter, laughing.

I'm going to nominate him for the Academy Award.

At home, I slipped in the back door. My wife shrieked and threw an apple pan dowdy at the ceiling, the youngest boy ran out of the room and put his head under the sofa pillow, and the dog, daringly, tried to nip my ankle.

I threw the hat on the bed and a few minutes later learned why THAT'S unlucky.

The dog pulled it down, ripped off the band, chewed holes along one side and slobbered over the crown.

I don't think he liked it. Neither did I.

---

# O, SAY CAN YOU SING?

In Washington, D. C., Van Cliburn opened a concert with an unscheduled number usually heard just before prize fights—"The Star-Spangled Banner." Critics said it was the first time, aside from war-time, that an artist had begun with the National Anthem.

Americans are the most patriotic people, and the shyest about showing it, but there seems these days to be a renewed awareness of "The Star-Spangled Banner" abroad in the land—the flag and the song.

When President Eisenhower made a speech recently at Staunton in the front yard of Mary Baldwin College, I was hurrying along about five blocks away, late, when away in the distance the band began playing the National Anthem. Only two other people were on the street, a man and his boy, and the father stopped immediately, his hand on the boy's shoulder until the band finished playing, so distantly that the music came and went with the shifting of the strong breeze.

There are other songs easier to sing. In fact, it takes trained tenors to hit it right, and even some of them lose their nerve, or voice, amid "the rocket's red glare."

One day, riding alone on the highway, I decided to try and give the song my best effort and see what happened. I sprained a muscle in the back of my head. Only Americans would pick a National Anthem they couldn't sing comfortably.

More and more the National Anthem is being followed on programs by "God Bless America" which ANYBODY can sing. It's almost too easy. I mean no disrespect when I suggest that you could even teach it one of those talking dogs that used to plague old-time radio. The words are simple, too, reiterated petitions to bless America from the mountains to the prairies to the ocean white with foam.

The trouble is that I don't see mountains, prairies, and oceans white with foam. I tend to see Kate Smith. Most of us hung back from singing it at first because Americans shrink from being patriotic in public, but Kate pitched in and rang it out so roundly, so clearly, that she almost made it, as they say, OUR song, meaning Kate's and the rest of us.

But there's nothing soft or easy about "The Star-Spangled Banner," either words or music. It demands the best that's in us. The first stanza is really two, long rhetorical questions. There's a stateliness to it that won't give way to steamlining, and, of course, above everything, the thought of men and women who have given their lives to the country for which it stands.

I heard it sung, as never before, in a large luncheon hall in the Hotel Commodore in New York City, packed with businessmen who had come to hear and view Nikita Khrushchev, sitting at the head table.

The occasion opened with the orchestra's playing "The Star-Spangled Banner," and the businessmen pushed back their chairs and stood up, most of them eyeing Khrushchev.

Suddenly, without warning, without preparation, a man over at a corner table started singing the National Anthem with the orchestra. His companions looked at him, startled, then THEY began singing. It caught at the edges of tables around them, and finally EVERYONE was singing, including the waiters.

The strain of singing it in the first place, plus the community of emotion, made us all try to sing it in a full-throated roar. Some hit notes they would never achieve again. Many were crying.

Khrushchev spun his head around to his interpreter. What is it? What does it mean? The interpreter spread his hands. Who could convey to a dictator the meaning of freedom and America, wrapped up in a song?

# THE BATTLE UNDER THE CARROT BIN

The brightest boy in the neighborhood, the oldest in a family
of 10 kids, was the clerk in the old-time store.

His hours were easy to remember.

Six to six.

(I still get a faintly illicit feeling shopping for groceries at 8
o'clock at night, as if buying bootleg oatmeal.)

He wore a white apron, horn-rimmed glasses, a big black pencil
behind his ear, and a cowlick over his right eye. He bounded up
and down behind a long oak counter that ran the length of the
store, hooking down cereal boxes from an eight-foot shelf with
a pole like an elephant goad, catching a box deftly on the run and
sliding it backhanded down the counter toward you while he was
loping the other way to pull down and shag a pint of pickles.
A dare-devil operation. I only saw him miss once.

With a sack of flour.

Wiggling the black pencil furiously, he would tote up the items
in a long column on the brown paper bag. At home you checked
each item, out of sport, to catch him in a rare error, and out of
necessity because the country was in an inexplicable depression and
why didn't Mr. Hoover DO something?

I wouldn't presume to run a check behind the addition of today's
cash register. Even if I discovered a slip, I'd be afraid to take it
up with the machine. It might hit me.

You went to THE STORE and it would have been disloyal to
go anywhere else. None of this impulse buying, whipping over
to the other side of town to pick up fresh asparagus. Back there,
the other side of town might as well have been the other side of
the moon.

The other day a food salesman told me it won't be long before
you can drive up to a store, punch a button, and a whole week's
groceries will tumble out, neatly packaged according to each day's
planned menu. I was aghast.

All the memories of the old store swept over me:

The day the mastiff and the pit bull, yearning all their mean lives to get at each other, finally locked jaws under the carrot bin . . .

The Saturday afternoon the tarantula jumped out of a banana stalk . . .

The night the manager clouted a burglar and then fed him pork and beans because he was hungry . . .

Can the push button produce such as that?

---

# A TALE OF TWO UNCLES

A visiting Englishman, a writer for Punch, told me that what struck him as curious about Americans was our fixation on weight. It seemed screamingly funny to him that even in our novels a character's weight is recorded as gravely as the color of his eyes and that on our wanted posters in the postoffice the criminal's weight is given as 168 pounds, as if, he said, you Americans were going to maneuver the culprit on the scales before you summoned the constabulary.

You watch weight with the same dedication that we British watch birds, he said.

I wrote him off as a blithering idiot until I began to focus on a day's ordinary talking, here and there, and sure enough, weight is the cruising gear of this country's conversation. It even beats the weather. Half my friends. I found, were on diets and wanted to tell you all about it, and the other half wanted to hold you by the lapels and explain why they were NOT on diets.

Housewives used to swap recipes. Now they exchange reducing formulas. During my boyhood, amid the flickering shadows of the Depression, what worried everybody was where the next meal was coming from. Now the concern is all where it's going to.

Back there you were fat or thin, and there was no great hullabaloo about it, either way. You had a thin Uncle and a fat Uncle.

The thin Uncle, George, was tall and serious and talked with you about your future and brought home stamps from his office mail for your collection.

The fat Uncle, Bob, was like a roaring, snapping fire that filled the room with mirth. Bob came bearing things to eat he had picked up at the open market on his way from work.

He would stride into the house, his face hidden from view behind huge brown sacks of groceries, his laughter and stray golden oranges bouncing and rolling around the room, his beautiful white Spitz dogs in a lather of activity around his feet, out of genuine love from Uncle Bob and the soup bone in the bottom of the bag.

Life with Uncle George was a mission. With Uncle Bob, it was a picnic.

It would have been confusing if the fat Uncle had lost weight and the thin Uncle had gained it. Then you would have had only uncle Uncles, a real deprivation for any child.

---

# WHAT HENRY DID

Someone gave my boys a valentine kit, and watching them clip and paste I remembered what my friend Henry did in the fourth grade.

What happened to Henry? He fell for the prettiest girl in the class. He stopped working on the tree hut. He did strange unheard of things, like hauling ashes out of the neighbors' basements for money.

On the way to school on Valentine's Day he bought the biggest valentine ever made, so big he could barely hide it in his blue-lined tablet with the horse head on the front cover. I throw in that horse head to show you how the day was branded on my memory.

He asked the teacher, first thing, if he could be postman. She was so shocked, at Henry wanting to do ANYTHING, she said yes.

The girls, giggling, placed on the teacher's desk a big soup carton covered with snow-white crepe paper and blood-red hearts. Everybody but Henry dropped in valentines. He walked up and down the aisles, calling out names, handing out valentines.

Henry, said the teacher, you can put down that tablet while you deliver the mail.

But he kept it under his arm, taking no chances, waiting for the moment to take the valentine from his tablet and hand it to the prettiest girl, a topper to the heap of plain and fancy hearts on her desk.

As the stack on her desk mounted, it became more and more noticeable that one girl in the class wasn't getting any.

Not even a comic.

She was out of school more than she was in, which was why she had been forgotten, and even when present, she was sullen, withdrawn, a regular briar patch.    Now she sat stiffly, looking straight ahead, her desk bare of a single envelope.  I could almost feel the tears in her eyes in my own.

Henry went right on, through all the growing embarrassment, delivering the mail.  Nothing ever threw Henry.  I knew him.

He stopped at his own desk and went to erasing and scribbling on what was in his tablet.

Now comes the big one, I thought.

Henry marched down the aisle, HIS valentine in his hand, right toward the prettiest girl in the class—and PAST her until he stood before the briar patch.

Here, he said, take it.

The briar patch looked unbelieving, at the huge envelope he was holding out to her.  She took it, her hand trembling.

Open it, he said, as if he'd like to punch her in the nose.

Boy, I thought.  Good ole Henry.  My pal.  But what a razzing he's going to take when the class finds he sent it.

Who's it from?  Who's it from? the girls were screaming.

She opened the envelope, look inside the valentine, and, turning to ME, she cried, through her tears, How can I ever, ever thank you?

That's what Henry did.

---

# THE MYTH THAT RUTH BUILT

As you know, this column usually treats of deep intellectual subjects—nuclear fission, the exploding universe, and all that—but today I'd like to explore another sphere, Babe Ruth.

How the rest of my family feels was pretty well summed up at breakfast when I asked the 8-year-old whether he would like to see the Babe's record of 60 home runs broken this season, and he said, through a mouthful of scrambled eggs, No, not unless Mantle breaks it.

My own feelings were given away the other evening when I asked at the supper table: Well, how did Babe Ruth do today? . . . as if he were still here.

I've been running a poll (very scientific, I simply ask everybody I meet) and find that all above 40 would prefer the Babe's record to stand, those between 20 and 40 split 50-50, and those under 20 are pulling for Maris or Mantle, with the majority favoring Mantle.

That those above 40 might be deciding the issue on the mere accident of age was disturbing until the reason came to me, lying in bed an extra 15 minutes this morning, the time when I do my heaviest thinking.

It's not just a conservative doting on things old, not just that we would like to see the mightiest record in baseball stand untouched by time, like Keats' Grecian Urn. The fact is, we are nearer the magical, moonlike pull of the Babe's giant personality.

The ingredients were three: his sometimes appalling honesty, a friendliness that make every one "keed" to him, and the sheer prodigal ability to hit home runs with—and this is what counts most— boyish gusto.

It was not only that he hit home runs. It was HOW he hit them. Fame set him apart from the rest of his team (though ballplayers trailed him like ordinary fans to see what he would do next), and one of his managers hated Ruth because the Babe succeeded blithely without having to knuckle under to rules made for lesser players.

That, at bottom, is why the every day eight-to-five clock-puncher gloried in the Babe. He did what all of us wish to do, secretly. He pulled off his feats in defiance of the established order and stole a little Promethean fire to warn the hearts of the pluggers who have to go by the book He kicked convention in the seat of the pants.

He didn't come to terms with the world, but baby-like went on and lived as he pleased and made the world like it. The owners had to change the game—hopping up the ball, building larger parks —to suit HIM. He did it all without thought, without bothering to figure out why. He did it, just as a natural, baseball's Paul Bunyan.

You find his like in other fields, American folk heroes with over-powering talent who went their own way in the face of bleak society and the law of averages . . . Davy Crockett, Mark Twain, Henry Ford.

The European is hedged and cribbed by tradition, going back centuries. The American feels, at times, as if he's walking under a lonely sky, on his own, with nothing much behind him and very little ahead of him except the horizon moving back.

The Babe solved it for himself—and others shared it, watching —by knowing or caring absolutely nothing for yesterday's tradition or today's celebrity. He was his own man. He created his own myth exuberantly.

Mike Houston, working for The New York Evening Post, covered the Babe for three years. One time Ruth remarked care-lessly that he couldn't go somewhere with some pals because he had to go to dinner with "those movie people." It could have been anybody, says Houston, cameramen or a girl Babe picked out of a ticket booth, but, investigating, his teammates found that "those movie people" were Doug Fairbanks and Mary Pickford.

Again, some of the Yankee team went to the White House to meet FDR, and when Babe reached him, the President told how, running for Governor of New York, he was gratified one evening to find a large crowd gathered at his hotel, only to see that their backs were turned to him. They're waiting to see Babe Ruth, somebody explained to him.

The President threw back his head to laugh at the memory, and Babe Ruth said, Yeah, that's the way it always is.

And always will be, no matter who breaks 60 and how often.

---

# SANTA DIESELIZED

The two older boys being involved Saturday in projects as extensive as Boulder Dam, I took the youngest, 5, on the Santa Claus train, a new experience for both of us.

When the three are together, there is a constant, whirling tracery of action, and the youngest, egged on by his older brothers, is the most in motion, the clown at whose antics the other two collapse in laughter.

Saturday, riding to Ashland on the train, he sat quietly, very straight in his seat. From time to time, smiling broadly, he would cut his eyes at me, and I would grin back, both of us on the verge of laughter, pleased with the occasion and with the spectacle of his own exemplary conduct, more humorous than if he had been vaulting around in his usual style.

There were various fine diversions—clowns, pretty teen-agers passing out candy canes, and a trip down the aisle for water—but they shrank to nothing when, passing through Ashland, we caught a fleeting glimpse of Santa and the beautiful Snow Queen standing and waving on the campus of Randolph-Macon College.

There was an empty red sleigh near them, and I was bracing myself to explain the absence of reindeer when he swung around and asked, accusingly: Where's his hat?

What hat?

He dint have a hat.

Listen, I said. He didn't even have any reindeer and here you are hollering about a hat. Ask HIM where his hat is when he comes through here.

The train sat on the tracks while Santa worked his way through 21 cars toward the two of us still arguing about his hat and whether it made any difference in the big picture.

There was a squeal in the car that overlaid all the other squeals. Leaning out of my seat and looking back through the doors into the car behind, I saw Santa coming down the aisle, reduced by the distance and the windows in successive car doors to a figure as compact as that on a Christmas seal, as if seen through the wrong end of a telescope. I grabbed the five-year-old and pointed out the approaching figure all ablaze in red satin. The boy took one look, pulled away, and sat tensely looking out his window.

Just behind us was a grandmother with as many children in tow as an old speckled dominicker hen. When Santa reached her brood, an intense look of concentration came over her face, and, her mouth slightly open, she repeated to herself everything he was saying to her charges. I was thinking how foolish that was until I realized I was repeating after HER.

When our turn came, I seized the boy and swung him around as if focusing a camera. Santa's broad, kindly face hovered over him, and the boy's face went rapt.

Riding back to Richmond, we discussed the speed of the train, the mechanism of the seat, and why the window wouldn't raise. The trip, I decided, had been a smasher.

When we got home, his two brothers swooped upon him, demanding to know what Santa Claus was like.

He dint have a hat, said the five-year-old.

---

# A VERY NEARLY PERFECT DAY

The bold sun swung across the blue sky, stark as an arc light. It was a very nearly perfect day on the beach.

There were not many people on the beach, because, to tell you the truth, there is not much of a beach, just about six feet of shore line full of driftwood, dead fish, and other curios to intrigue the boys.

At one point, however, the beach fails to make a turn and overshoots the mainland in a sandbar long as five city blocks and about two lanes wide. It glides into the sea so gradually that you can wade out more than a block, feeling as if you could walk to the horizon, the white water roiling around your ankles over both sides of the sandbar. The boys call it, as if it were something cataclysmic, "the place where the waters meet."

They tore ahead, running out on the sandbar to the head of the point, bent on scaring a flock of gulls that rose screaming in white lattice work against the sky, so that, running, flinging their arms far out on the point, the boys seemed to be climbing with them.

Along the way half a dozen persons were surfcasting, as good an excuse as any for loafing, if you've got a conscience that won't let you lie down friddell-like and soak in the sun.

We passed a group of lounging teen-agers spread cart-wheel, their heads around a tiny transistor radio which was playing Glenn Miller's Tuxedo Junction.

Plodding past, I overheard one of them say, clearly, "Schlemiel."

Did you hear that? I asked my wife. They just called Tuxedo Junction schlemiel.

Are you sure they were talking about Tuxedo Junction? she asked.

Tuxedo Junction was "our" song, a whole generation's about to go to war, and now, as I passed, it sounded a little tired even to me. I don't like rock and roll, I can't enjoy Aida, and now, after 20 years, Tuxedo Junction, seems predictable  What a schlemiel.

The boys leaped gleaming brown and limber in the white surf, their heads bobbing dark as seals against the wind-banked waves. Sometimes I joined them, but most of the time I sprawled in the sun on the sand.  After all, I told my wife, Isaac Newton discovered gravity when he was lying under an apple tree.  Maybe I shall find hilarity.

On the way back, the boys again tore along in front, running past the parked car and on down the beach road ahead of us, the idea being to see how far they could get before we reached them in the car, aiming to set a new record for distance.

The youngest, the 6-year-old, coat-hanger thin from always trying to keep up with his two older brothers, has yellow hair and a zany grin like Harpo Marx.  Taking a turn, we saw him in the distance, as he put on a wild spurt, his legs twinkling like a Keystone comedy chase, arms flailing, staggering wildly when he looked back at the approaching car, laughing so that he could hardly breathe, the sunlight caught in his curly head.

One other thing happened, while we were still lounging in the sun.  A teen-ager came over and told us there had just been a news flash that the East Germans were sealing the Berlin border, and the United States was protesting vigorously.  I told you, it was a very nearly perfect day on the beach.

---

# ON TURNING 40

A teen-ager I know told his history teacher that he would just as soon pass out of the picture when he reaches 40 because by THAT time you have done everything, and there's nothing left to do but work.

They got into this by way of a discussion of glaciers, and Rick's parents relayed his observation to me because I just turned 40. We knew you would appreciate it, said his father, who is going to be 40 himself in two months, so why is he so gleeful at my plight?

That's the point. You never quite believe you are to be 40 until you wake one morning and are no longer 39. Too late, then, to turn back and do all the things you were going to do "before I get to be 40." Now I am beginning to wonder if I ever really will explore the Amazon. Or even the Orinoco.

In childhood every birthday is a bright explosion of ribbons and tissue paper—pink, white and blue but then the excitement tapers off until a birthday is only an almost imperceptible rise in the tide of years, about as memorable as National Asparagus Day. There are a few highwater birthdays . . . 13, 16, 21, 65 . . . but 40 stands out as the great watershed in a man's years.

Walter B. Pitkin wrote a book, "Life Begins at 40," but the very fact that it sold so well reflects the mild, fleeting apprehension most of us feel at crossing that dateline. I prefer Tennyson's outlook—that every hour is a bringer of new things—and I feel blithe as a boy of 10, but what bothers me is how OTHER people regard 40, particularly the bosses in the world of business.

Out in Chicago last week a psychiatrist said there's an irrational tendency on the part of industry to regard the 40's as the years when a person settles down and ceases to show daring. This is unfortunate because the latter half of a man's career can more likely be even more productive, said the psychiatrist (who had just turned 40, no doubt.)

One of the nation's freedoms you don't hear much about is the right to resign and move about freely in seeking new work. (In Russia a man has to go through a mountain of red tape just to quit and then get a passport to look for work in the next town.)

There's much attention on the right-to-work, but let's not overlook the right NOT to work, the right to quit and tell the boss to go jump in the James, the right to move on, as Daniel Boone did, every time he heard a rooster crow or saw the neighbors' smoke. Often, when the bills get higher, the going seems rough, and the way is no clearer than it was at the start, there's consolation in the thought: Well, you can always quit.

But do I feel near as much like quitting this month at 40 as I did last month at 39? Do the bosses really believe they have got us at 40?

On my birthday, riding up on the elevator, my boss, just as the doors were closing, called in a friendly way, Happy Birthday, Friddell!

By George, I thought, what did he mean by THAT? That was a cryptic remark, if I ever heard one. Happy birthday, huh? He never did that before!

I had half a mind to go in and resign.

But I didn't. Chickened out at 40.

---

# HOW IT WARS IN HAWAII

An occasional balmy day reminds me of Hawaii where my out-fit, the strangest that ever pulled KP, spent a portion of World War II.

Strange that you should feel home-sick, briefly, for a place in in which you were home-sick most of the time. What made Hawaii's paradise so appalling was the fact that any of us would have swapped it for a worked-out coal mine back home.

It was a lotus land. There was no Winter, no Summer, no Fall, just a mild, smiling, perpetual Spring except for a month or so of rainy season in which you got a year's rain at one shot. The island is just one big mountain rising from the sea depths. Its slopes are covered, fold on fold, with suger cane, lush, green, deep —as if a giant tidal wave were washing up its sides.

We lived in the barracks of a former sugar plantation sur-rounded by cane fields. The rain would come marching across those cane fields, and you could hear its steady rush a half-minute away. Then the rain would break upon the tin roofs of the buildings with a double-fisted roar that could drown out a thousand snare drums. If the gray scythe of rain ever reached you, it drenched a well-pressed khaki uniform in a second.

Animals were conditioned to it, and even before you heard the rain, you'd see the dogs and cats streak into a run for cover. A few seconds later you would hear the rain coming through the cane fields like a fast-rushing express. I got so that when I saw a dog running, I'd run, too.

One Saturday morning before inspection, afraid to sit down and ruin the crease in my pants, I was walking around the area when I saw a dog running around the corner of the headquarters building. Instinctively, I took off after the dog, guessing that he must be headed for the nearest shelter, and the two of us went galloping around the corner, the dog in the lead.

As we cleared the corner, I saw that the dog was chasing a cat, and coming toward all three of us was the Colonel in command of our outfit, a sad-eyed man who looked like Robert E. Lee without a beard. That's how we were lined up, dog, cat, and Friddell, on a dead run at the Colonel who looked like Lee. By George, I thought, this IS a dilemma. How can I explain to the Colonel that I started chasing this dog to get out of the rain when the dog is all too obviously chasing a cat?

I just kept right on running, straight by the Colonel, looking neither right nor left like the Charge of the Light Brigade slightly reduced and going in the wrong direction, just veering about two degrees so I wouldn't bump into the Colonel with sad eyes. We almost scraped as I shot by. Going away, about 50 feet off, I risked a glance backwards at the Colonel. He was running, too.

That's how it was in Hawaii, in the outfit I was in anyway.

---

# IT WAS SOAPORIFIC !

A colleague was telling me that he and his wife visited her home town this Summer, and he chanced to drop in on the middle of a conversation that appalled him.

The women in the gathering were talking excitedly about stark and sordid events in the lives of what he took to be fellow towns-people because all the women—even his wife—knew them by their first names.

He sat there, heart-stricken at the recital of what was taking place in one little town in Southside Virginia, enough trouble to fill a big city, when suddenly one of the girls referred to "today's episode" and he realized that all along they had been re-hashing television soap operas. He wobbled out of the room, he said, and only the sight that night of gruff old Cheyenne restored his perspective.

It was the second such shock television had handed him, he said. For weeks his wife had been urging him to come home to lunch once in a while, so one day, being out in the neighborhood, he stopped by home and found her sitting, eating lunch avidly before the television set.

She waved a fork at him to be quiet, and seeing that he couldn't compete for her attention with Linda Storm—or some such turbulent name— he went out in the kitchen and made a peanut butter and banana sandwich, only as he couldn't find the mayonnaise, he used mustard and was sick the rest of the day. That's what Linda Storm did to ME, he said.

An even bolder bid came last Tuesday night when after TV's trying to mesmerize women half the day with soap operas, one soap company went pseudo-intellectual and presented a program —"The Trapped Housewife"—aimed at convincing women that all of them, the viewers, were trapped in what amounted to a gigantic soap opera, life.

The narrator—a lady with a strong jaw and slide-rule eyebrows, the kind of a face that makes me feel guilty even before she opens her mouth—said that "millions of American women who answer to the name of 'housewife' (she spat that last word) had a new occupational disease called the disenchantment syndrome," a trapped feeling that leads them to wonder "Is this all? Is there more to life than being a good wife or a good mother?"

Strong Face said that the average housewife spent nine and a half years of her life washing dishes and 15 years preparing meals, but she did not say how much time they spent looking at Linda Storm.

The distraught housewife said she used to look forward to wanted the right "to say no to a good home, a washing machine, and a good neighborhood." Perhaps, right there, her non-plussed husband should have presented her a ribbed washboard and a galvanized iron tub and returned the washing machine on which he was probably having trouble meeting the payments anyway.

The distraught housewife said she used to look forward to having lunch with the men in the office. Where I work, some of us open brown paper bags and eat sandwiches prepared by our trapped mates and others step downstairs to Mr. Kirby's for an impossibly romantic hot dog and coffee.

I could criticize this program all day, but the only quote that really distressed me occurred when the trapped housewife, referring to her children, said sometimes she felt that she did nothing but "live in a world of people three feet high," as unfeeling a designation for children as I've heard in a long time.

The program was a soap-slick contrivance, dishwater. I was relieved that my wife saw it as phony because if it had been pitched the same way at a male audience, I'd have taken the bait before it hit the water and gone to bed sobbing in self-pity.

There's not another day or civilization in which women have done as much creatively as they do now. I see them enriching the community constantly— running Main Street offices, insisting that legislators do right by our schools and mental hospitals, acting in plays, leading community drives, working in the church.

Of course, any of us, off and on, feels caught in a rut, but it's a luxury to be so situated that you have the breath to feel trapped. Most of the time we are weaving and dodging through one bewildering combination after another so that a rut would be welcome in the day's minefield of challenges.

Anyway, all the minor annoyances, the frustration of seeming to jump two steps, and fall back one, fade in the face of an illness or accident involving someone close, or even someone unknown on whose ill fortune we read and grieve.

The truth is, life is intolerably sweet and brief, and if we wish to deaden our sense occasionally to its swift, dazzling passage, then I guess that television is as good a dope as any.

## POPS' CONCERT

It's called a pops concert because all the children ask their pops for soda pop.

Up until half-time, there's an exciting mixture of rousing music and liniment smells from the basketball games which are also held in the Richmond Arena. The orchestra plays under the south basket.

Then at the half a great children's chorus arises from the stands, and it goes like this:
I'M THIRSTY!
Over and over.

Last time, as I set out for soft drinks, my wife said, Why not let the three boys go along?

I could think of a thousand reasons why not, but she anticipated them all, by saying, Oh, go on, be a sport.

That's how we came to be jammed in a mass before the drink stand with just little eddies in the crowd to mark my three. I hauled them into the open air where we were recovering when along came the wife of a fellow reporter, also bent on buying soft drinks for her brood. Look, I said, you watch my three, and I'll go back in there and buy for all of us.

She needed five drinks, and I figured that by holding two open cups in each hand, balancing two on the shoulders, two on the knees, one on my head, hopping along with one on the instep, and whistling Dixie, I could just about make it, if the wind held.

Draped in drinks, I was moving out of the crowd, apologizing to right and left, when the counterman called: STOP THAT MAN WITH THE DRINK ON HIS HEAD.

I could have sworn I'd paid him.

I inched back to the counter, and he said, Here's your three cents change.

Keep 'em, I said.

Not allowed to, he said.

Then put 'em in my mouth.

WHAT?

I said PUT-THE-PENNIES-IN-MY-MOUTH.

I turned to another customer and said, By George, you'd think he could understand a simple request like that.

Sure, sure, said the other customer, edging away, bumping the wall of people around us.

Put the pennies in his mouth, he advised the counterman. Do anything he says.

The counterman did, and let me say it's been nigh on 30 years since I've tasted a penny, and they don't taste one bit better.

All coppery.

I edged out of the crowd, spilling only two drinks, and there on the outskirts were my friend, my three boys and two dancing little girls. I gave each little girl a drink, and they thanked me prettily and disappeared.

Those are certainly nice little girls, I said.

I thought so, too, she said. But they aren't mine.

With argument, to the tuning up of the orchestra, I pressed five of the drinks upon her, and then the boys and I returned to the stands escorting the last cup. My wife raised an eyebrow but made no comment.

Boys, boys, I said, we're going to play a little game called marooned-on-a-desert-island-with-but-one-cup-of-pop. Starting with your mother, we'll each take a sip, and be sure some is left at the end OR GUYBO WILL GO OUT OF HIS HEAD WITH THIRST.

Honey, asked my wife, why are you talking so funny?

It's those dad-burned pennies I ate, I said.

Oh, she said. I should have known.

---

# THAT'S THE WAY THE TREE FALLS

In putting up the Christmas tree there are at least three areas of debate, as they say in the UN. One school of thought—my wife —says Santa should put up the tree at about 2 o'clock on Christmas morning, finishing only an hour or two before the children come rushing into the room. Their faces are something to see, she said.

I can't I replied. I'm too bushed. Along towards the last I can't even see the tree.

One Christmas dawn I decorated a blue armchair with a whole pack of icicles. Then tried to sit in the tree.

The second topic is how to put on the icicles. She believes in arranging them one by one, as if setting a table. My system is to stand off and fire away, Gridley like.

But the basic decision in selecting a tree or a Secretary of State is whether you want a "modest" one, in her words, a self-effacing sort on the order of Dean Rusk, or a great big rollicking extrovert along the lines of Chester Bowles, that won't even let you in the room.

I lean to a bold tree, but because she agreed Saturday to let the tree go up early, I scaled down my demands on its size.

That's how democracy works, the old give and take, I told the three boys as we drove to get the tree at the neighborhood lot.

As you drive through the countryside, any bush on the side of the road looks perfect for a role in the littlest Christmas tree. In lots, stood in rows or piled in heaps, they all look alike. You cannot see the trees for the forest. The only tree I see I want is one somebody else is already hauling away.

Finally, we picked one and took it home, the smallest tree we'd had in 14 years, so modest it almost simpered, but it had a mean streak, a Uriah Heep of a tree.

It wouldn't stand straight. Half an hour went by before the youngest boy discovered a bend halfway up the trunk.

Then the trunk wouldn't slip through the ring on the tree stand because of knots that I had to saw away with the bread knife.

Finally, the confounded props on the stand kept sliding off the trunk which was too small. As a last supreme effort, the better to work two props at once I lay on my back on the rug, with the stand and the trunk of the upright tree resting on my stomach, roaring instructions to the three boys to stop dancing around, dash it, and hold up the tree, I adjure you, HOLD-UP-THE-TREE!!

Over she went.

Be happy it wasn't a Sequoia, I told my wife, as she sorrowed over the lamp.

This tree doesn't like me, I added. Anyway, the trunk is too small.

We traded it in on another, a joyous number, so bountiful it overflows the room. We have to conduct guided tours through it to get into the kitchen. Gazing at it, my wife said wistfully, Some Christmas I'd like to have a really small, modest tree.

That's how democracy works, I told her. You have to make concessions.

I can't wait to throw on the icicles.

# A TIGER ON THE FAR WALL

Barbers are a lot speedier than they used to be. Where a haircut now takes 15 or 20 minutes, it used to take three hours and a half. Conservatively.

I have known a haircut to take an entire Saturday, the thought of it hanging there in the back of your mind from the moment you got up, a pall on an otherwise green gold day. Finally, about 3 p.m. when the heat hovered over the tar street—it is a funny thing, but I do not ever remember getting a haircut in the Winter, only on a hot Saturday afternoon when I should have been wading sensibly in a creek—the barber fitted a board across the arms of the chair, and you climbed up on the board, pressing your knee, as you did, against the sun-warmed leather of the seat.

There was a big overhead fan circling around on the ceiling, so slowly that flies had time to loop in and out of its beat and even ride on the blades when they got tired. All the barber's tools, too, were in the nature of insects that buzzed, and snipped and snapped, and crawled, munching up the back of your neck.

The keenest torture was the slow, thousand-footed passage of time, an inch-worm crossing the Sahara. You sat there, the black and white striped sheet just short of choking you on the spot, while the glorious world of Saturday spun away just beyond the prison's plate glass front.

Sometimes you could steal a glance at the golden stage of the outside world across which a delivery boy passed, idling deliciously, on his bicycle, the spokes of the turning wheels all interwoven with strips of blue, pink, and white crepe paper, the sun rolling around gaudily on the earth, while you sat a prisoner in the dock. It was almost as bad as school.

Generally, though, when the barber saw you peeking toward the window, he would swing you around to face the lattice-work near the ceiling along the rear of the shop, or to stare, mesmerized, at the chair's dull silver foot rest on which a single word—Koken —was still legible in the center of the worn pig-guts scroll-work.

On the far wall, posted over the mirror, was an advertisement

for something called "Lucky Tiger" that promised: "Cures Dandruff or Money Back." I was a little uncertain as to exactly what
sort of dread disease " money back" might be, but it sounded considerably worse than dandruff. I had a mental picture of money
—silver dollars—forming in scales along a person's backbone, and
I hoped I'd never catch the stuff.

One day, years later, lying on a canvas cot on a Pacific island
on a hot Saturday afternoon, wishing I were home, in much the
same mood that used to overcome me in the barber's chair, I suddenly saw in my mind the "Lucky Tiger" placard and it said not
"Money Back" but "Money . . . back."

I went to sleep, smiling.

---

# DOUBLE RAINBOW

If I ever get $100 ahead, I shall quit and go be a beachcomber.
On second thought, that would be foolish. I shall simply lie on the
beach and let other people do the combing. Turn me over as you
go by, I'll tell them. Days like this, I'm like that.

The first day the thermometer climbed above 50 I shouted to
the family, Get set! We're going on a picnic in the sunshine.

In the rain, don't you mean? asked my wife. Have you looked
at the clouds?

Fakes, I said, and off we went, all five, to a big picnic table
near the river where three remarkable things happened.

First off, there came a rushing noise, as of heavy wind in the
trees.  What looked like a solid wall of rain broke out of the
woods and came toward us.

Run for the car, cried my wife.

We'll never make it, I shouted. UNDER THE TABLE,
everybody!

Thinking all the time (the old brain never stops ticking, I told
my wife later), I pulled the charcoal grill under the table along
with us. It was like being in the bottom of the ocean in a leaky
bathysphere. Under the table the silence was sodden.

Boys, boys, I shouted. Where's the old pepper? This is really roughing it. Much better than television. Pretend we're in a prairie schooner surrounded by Indians.

The rain's soaking the hamburgers, said my wife.

Sure enough, little rivers were pouring through the chinks in the table. I humped over the grill to shield it, crouched on all fours above the hot, glowing coals while the cold rain sluiced down my back.

By George, I said, this is as near as I ever expect to come to being baked and basted in one operation.

Watch your feet, said my wife. The water's coming in from the side now.

At last the rain roared on down the river to find other picnics. We came out from under the table. The sun came out, too, and the landscape shone wetly golden as if a tingling green paint brush had swept it.

While we were standing, like Noah waiting to dry, there appeared the other two remarkable things, rainbows for the spirit.

A train thundered by, just across the canal, and the engineer, grinning, hurried to the other side of his cabin to give us a long honk on the  diesel horn.

Just after that, a large deer, forest gray, came running down the slope of the hill, and, seeing us, paused, frozen, then bounded off in a rocking motion across the green hill until he blended in the woods.

Rain, a deer . . . and the train.

Two for one. Not bad for a picnic.

---

# ON THE BEACH . . . BEANS

To one side on the beach was a pile of canned goods, with no labels, and on the other was our outfit of 300 or so, with nothing to eat since the night before.

Between us stood Sergeant Maypop his fists on his hips.

None of yers, he bellowed, is going to touch one of these cans. The stuff could be contaminated, and before I let yers eat, I'LL KILL YERS.

The sergeant was a big man, so big that when he walked he looked like a parade with a bass drum out front.

His voice was so powerful it could bounce off high clouds. His feelings were so tender that when anybody had to swat a fly, he left the room.

We were seated, most of us, on our helmets, like a community of khaki clad flamingos trying to hatch olive drab eggs on the lonely beach under the dank sky. Nobody knew where we were. We were lost.

Or rather, our officers got into the wrong boats, getting off the ship, and THEY were lost, and we didn't know where to go. The second our feet touched the sand, Sergeant Maypop lightning-like, had us sit down and wait.

At dusk a jeep came careening down the beach, and standing up in it was the youngest lieutenant in our outfit, leaning way out and waving his hand at us, as if he were flagging down a runaway train.

Where have you guys BEEN? he asked the sergeant who just saluted and looked green.

There's trucks waiting a mile down the beach, said the lieutenant. Get to it. ON THE DOUBLE. It's going to rain, he added, as it began to rain.

On the double, as we passed the pile of cans, I scooped one up.

The trucks ground along through the darkness and a drumming downpour to a hillside where we fell out and began trying to put up pup tents in pairs in the roaring rain. My partner Wes, was big, steady, even-tempered, even when the tent fell on us, like wet wash, every half hour.

In one pause, I said, Wes, I've got one of those contaminated cans in my pack.

Get it out, he said.

We hacked it open, up-ended it over a mess kit, and out fell pork and beans. He found a little fuel block, and lit it. The beans began to simmer and bubble. Just watching warmed our innards. Wes went to rummaging in the back of the tent.

Hurry, I said. The beans are ready.

I can't find my spoon, he said.

Use mine, I said. I'll lap 'em up.

No, said Wes, we're going to eat in style.

I put the beans down and leaned back to help look for the spoon. He turned around. I hate to tell you this, he said.

Tell me what? I asked.

Your feet are in the beans, he said.

We sat and shivered and thought of how good the beans had smelled.

They were probably contaminated, said Wes.

ARE YOUSE GUYS HUNGRY?

The voice almost blew over the tent again. Sergeant Maypop's moon face peered through the flap.

He led us through walls of rain to a large-size cook tent, packed with men, all of them eating. Beans.

I sent a truck for that pile on the beach, said the Sergeant, ladling beans onto my mess kit.

How do you know they're not contaminated? I asked.

Ate a can myself, he said. And I feel fine. He beat his chest. FINE! he said.

Gulping the beans, I looked over at Wes staring down at his filled mess kit.

What's the matter with you? I asked.

No spoon, he said.

---

# ALL-AMERICAN HALF-TIME HALF-BACK

Have you ever noticed, when you enter the crowded stands at a football game, how nobody knows you, not even your creditors? You look, vainly for some kind of soul to arise and shout: Hey, ole sport! Up here! Two fine seats.

I have nightmares of wandering around interminably in a football stadium looking for a seat, under the cold stares of the crowd. You are about as popular as Marie Antoinette making her way to the guillotine.

The tide turns during half-time. The band is out there, playing bravely, forming strange new letters in the alphabet, and you struggle to your feet and ask your wife, casually, How about a coffee?

Her answer is lost in glad shouts of recognition from all over the stadium. Magically, the stands are filled with your friends, all hungry.

How about bringing back 18 coffees, yells one—three with cream and no sugar, nine with sugar and no cream, three black with sugar, and three with sugar, and no black.

From the other side comes another request: Hey, ole horse, bring us 32 pronto pups, will ya?—12 with mustard, 8 without, four with mustard and relish, but no catchup; seven with relish and catchup, but no mustard, and two without anything.

(If that doesn't add, so it didn't out at the Stadium either.)

The pronto pup is a new-style hot-dog, dipped on a stick into boiling batter, then dabbed with dressing. It's no mean trick to dab a pronto pup with relish—and make it stick.

You tight-rope back through the crowd, a slowly moving, human grape-fruit stuck with tooth-pick hors-d'oeuvres, apologizing as you smear the big guy in the camel's-hair coat.

No harm done, sir, just a touch of red and yellow at your shoulders. That's popular in Paris this year. Don't hit me or I might explode and start a third world war.

The pronto pups are delicious . . . I guess.

I never had one.

Somewhere along the line, at one of the stops in the stands, a girl has come in late, wearing a yellow chrysanthemum and a wide-painted smile, her cheeks flushed a delicate pink with hunger. The gay, blithe spirit of autumn, as the poets say, gets the last pronto pup.

I suppose my progress through the stands is an irresistible picture. Clown-like even—a pudgy joker, giant pronto pups sprouting paddle-fingered from his mitts. I wouldn't blame strangers for laughing.

What hurts is when your friends, the very persons who sent you, rock in mirth and pass gay witticisms.

Hey! Look at the showboat, willya!

What a clown won't do for attention!

What does he think he is?

I know what I am.

An All-American half-time halfback.

# BY JET TO L. A.

LOS ANGELES
July 10, 1960

Dear Gin:

There's nothing like a jet flight across America with a clear, unobstructed view of the number two engine on the right wing. I may go into aeronautical engineering when I get home.

Riding with me on the aisle back in the tourist section (seating six abreast) on the way to the Democratic and Republican conventions was John Daffron of the Associated Press. Blocking the nearest porthole was a pale fellow reading Hegel.

Daffron. the coolest man I know on a fast-breaking story, looks like a distinguished junior diplomat but it frustrated him that we couldn't see out. Ever so often he would get out in the aisle and make a trout-like hungry leap, trying to peek out the porthole over Hegel's shoulder.

Once, when others were exclaiming at what was below, Daffron leaned across and tried to peer past our Hegelian.

Pardon me, he said, may I look at your ground?

The jet eased along with the low murmur of a well-bred air-conditioner, and Daffron pored over a map and announced what we were missing.

We should be over Tulsa about now, he said. Ask him if he he sees any derricks.

Excuse me, I said, but do you see any derricks down there?

He stopped reading and looked down.

Only an arroyo, he reported.

What did he say he saw? asked Daffron.

Arroyo, I said.

I'm fine, said Daffron. How're you?

Look how blue the sky is up here, I said, pointing to a shoulder patch at the porthole.

It clashes with my suit, said Daffron, refusing to be consoled.

Just occasionally we caught sight of the rolling panorama below . . . fleecy cloud pastures . . . land laid out in neat rectangles of washed-out pink, green and ocher, like a child's clay set . . . a bare mountain range, the ridged backbone of a dinosaur crawled to his death.

I'd asked the stewardess if we are going over the Grand Canyon, murmured Daffron, only I'm sure she'd say, Whaddaya think . . . that we go under it?

A stewardess came toward us, smiling.

Ask her, I suggested.

Oh, Miss, called Daffron. Are we going over the Grand Canyon?

Why no, she, said, dimpling. This trip we're going under it.

But in less than a half hour the big plane wing dipped slowly, and we looked down . . . as if to the center of the earth.

Filling the windows in frozen silence were huge blind fingers of stone.

The pale fellow dropped his Hegel and let it lie when the plane righted itself.

What is there to say after the Grand Canyon?

Except . . .

Love,

Guybo

P. S.—I'm mailing you a Stevenson button over which to weep. The Democrats would nominate Adlai only if Ike were running and nobody could win.

---

# THE VOTE WATCH

LOS ANGELES, July 18.—Everything here is something else.

For a garden party in the hills a host carpeted his tennis courts with artificial grass.

The fine-sifted sunshine doesn't burn.

People crawl out of swimming pools as dry as if they were splashing in bright cellophane. I have not bothered to check. It must be cellophane.

The hotel lobbies appear doubly large because they are banked in mirrows. They are also dark, filled with bronze gloom or deep violet twilight.

The people too are fabulous.

Assigned as guides to each delegation were so-called Golden Girls, in uniforms of white dresses, blue or red sashes, and school-girl straw hats. They were sworn to be impartial in politics, but a careful questioning—such as hello—would show that to a girl they were for Adlai Stevenson.

During the howling demonstration for Stevenson in the convention hall, one Golden Girl raced up to the Virginia delegation, grabbed a dignified delegate by the lapels, and swinging him to and fro, tears streaking her blue eye-shadow, she cried:

"Isn't it terrible to want to do something terribly and not be able to because you must stay so terribly nonpartisan?"

In the same demonstration stalked a young man glum and silent. Why aren't you yelling? I asked, bending close to him in the hubbub.

I lost my voice booing the others, he croaked.

A woman marched by, holding one of those little dogs that looks like a kitten, plopped it into the arms of a startled Texan, and vanished into the crowd, calling, gaily, I'll be back.

Even those of us who weren't Los Angelenos tended to behave as they did.

In the rear concourse of the convention hall, a steep flight of broad steps led to the upper level of the building, steps broad as those in front of many high schools.

Almost any time more than 100 persons were massed on the steps while in the center a short, large-faced man called the roll of the caucus.

That's the Alabama delegation, someone said. They have to come out here every two hours and caucus.

The chairman would sound a man's name and the delegate would shout back: Lyndon B. Johnson, the next President of the United States.

That would draw applause, and the next one would shout, Adlai E. Stevenson, a prophet who shall not be without honor in the great state of Alabama.

More applause, even from those backing Lyndon, and so it went down the list of the candidates.

The Alabamans were holding their own, distinct convention in the back hallway.

The light, falling through the giant stairwell from above, was washed out, and the plain, gray faces in the faint light made me think of a Rembrandt grouping—the night watch, perhaps. Only this was a vote watch.

It happened over and over, the votes changing under pressure each time they returned to the hall until someone demanded another caucus out on the concourse.

Leaving L. A., I still hear those cotton-mouthed Alabama voices shouting their choice, and though I smile, it is in pride.

---

# THE ROCK AT WORK

CHICAGO, July 25.—There was a continuous feature here yesterday, running late into the night, named Nelson Rockefeller.

Today there's a double bill, with Richard Nixon arriving, and Rockefeller made the most of his last day on the stage alone.

I caught two of his five stops, the first at noon when the chunky dynamo pumped and purred his slightly nasal way through more than 2,000 packing the lobby and two fair-size ballrooms in the Hotel Sheraton Blackstone, Nixon's headquarters.

Rockefeller moved through the howling crowd, his shoulders slightly hunched as if in a pelting rain. Ever so often he pounced to one side to give someone a double handclasp, a gay wink, and a "so nice to see yew."

In his large, cliff-like face, his blue eyes are small, almost crossed. When he widens his lids to look at a person sharply, the effect is one of gazing into fast-clicking lenses.

In the ballroom he made an informal talk on the crucial times, through which the crowd lapsed largely into inattention, fans moving slowly on the surface like the gills of a listless fish.

As he finished and raised his arms, the audience roared to life again. One faded, middle-aged woman in a pink print, extended her hand timidly toward him, and before she could recover from her own half-impulse, Rockefeller reached out and grabbed it while still waving to the applause with the other hand.

As he moved back through the crowd, his mouth split into a big grin that never left his face, even in calling out greetings.

What appeals to the public is his image—and an occasional flashing idea—of a man who gets things done at a time in the world when something desperately needs doing. He moves decisively, even in his walk. He strides along, hands waist high, as if wading rapidly, hip-deep in water, going out purposefully after an errant beach ball.

A frequent gesture of his is a half-comic, helpess shrug, particulary when he is being escorted, with frequent sorties on his part, through frenzied admirers in a cordon of police. His shrug seems to say, appealing for understanding, I'd like-to-stay-but-they-are-pulling-me-away.

Another mannerism is the use of the word "fel-la," with a winsome lingering, a habit that must have galled Nixon when, after accusing him of ducking the issues, Rockefeller met him at a public function, clapped him on the back, and said, "Hi-ya, fel-la."

I picked up the show again yesterday at the Merchandise Mart, Chicago's largest building (owned by Sen. John Kennedy's father), where Rockefeller was to appear on Meet the Press.

He was ushering his staff people on the elevator, insisting they get on before him, assuring one and all there was room for everybody. I got on, too, drawing only a slightly abstract look.

Riding up, he flapped his coat over his wilted shirt and said his speech at the last stop had been choppy because of smear or mist on his glasses. Amid murmured reassurances from his staff, someone remarked that Sen. Barry Goldwater was to be on the program, too.

"Oh, Barry's going to be here? That's fine," Rockefeller exclaimed, as if Goldwater were a long lost cousin, not the man who had accused Rockefeller and Nixon of staging a GOP Munich in New York. Part of Rockefellar's charm is his conviction, pretty well-founded, that nobody can dislike him for long.

In the studio, Goldwater, his needle-sharp features stiff under pancake makeup, was told by his wife: "Don't smile too much."

"I can't," he said. "My face would crack."

Goldwater speaks with blunt, almost child-like naivete, one of the few members of the far-right wing with a light, witty touch

which the left wing likes to regard as its monoply.  Goldwater is
the Adlai Stevenson of the GOP old guard.

When Rockefeller's turn came, with 10 seconds to go, he wig-
wagged his eyebrows at his family, as if sending them encourage-
ment.

He was soft-spoken, serious.  He hunched forward, leaning on
his left elbow, his shoulder a big mass that could have pleased a
sculptor.

His stint done, he murmured to Lawrence Spivak, a member of
the TV panel, that he thought Barry had done very well but wasn't
so sure about himself.  He and Goldwater parted with what seemed
genuine affection.

On the way down, I asked Rockefeller's teen-age son, what was
the most amusing thing that had happened that day.

Without breaking stride, he said promptly, "This is trivial, but
I thought it most amusing when he squeezed a small dog.  Ironical-
ly, he hates dogs, generally, but this one was wearing a big draft
button, so I guess that was the deciding element."

Bounding to his limousine, Rockefeller saw a mother with two
small boys over to one side.  He strode over, introduced himself
to her, bowing slightly with his feet together as if a receiving line
had popped up on the pavement, then began questioning the boys.
He kept lingering, not quite satisfied, wishing somehow to round out
the situation and stamp it to his and their satisfaction, finally asking,
"What are you boys doing here?"

"Waiting to see you," blurted the younger one.

"O-o-oKAY-Y-Y-Y-Y," said Rockefeller, touseling his hair.
"You're nice boys."

He bounded into the car and it pulled away behind a screaming
motorcycle.  As far as we could see, he was looking back waving
at the mother, the two boys, and me, none of whom casts a single
delegate vote in the Chicago convention.

# STOCKYARD REVERIE

First thing that struck me on returning from the conventions in Chicago and Los Angeles was how weary everybody looked in Richmond.

No wonder, said my wife, they have been watching and listening to the conventions until all hours of the morning. Every day, she said, it was as if the whole city had stayed up for the late, late show.

At gatherings, this person and that has recalled exciting moments of the televised conventions while I stood by, silently, in awe.

Did you see the fight that almost broke out in the Connecticut delegation? somebody asked me.

I confessed that about that time I was sitting in Nixon's hospitality lounge in the Hotel Hilton with a tired couple from Pocatello watching "Meet McGraw."

It seems, I said, that this crooked count was breaking the house with phony dice and nobody could figure how, and old McGraw—

But they had seen that, too. It was a summer re-run.

All I have to offer today, in closing the subject, is a last scene that took place in the vast parking lot behind the Chicago hall.

I had wandered out into the musty red odor of the stockyards to escape the smoke-blue air of the amphitheater.

I was idling along when suddenly, behind a barricade of yellow sawhorses, as if marking the end of the road, there were, standing in loose array, 47 Uncle Sams, thick as Wordsworth's daffodils.

There were fat Uncle Sams, thin ones, tall and short, weathered looking Uncle Sams in the far sixties, young ones with only a peach fuzz on their cheeks, Uncle Sams everywhere. A poet could not but be gay in such a jocund company.

Each Uncle Sam wore red-and-white striped trousers, a blue swallow-tail coat, and a soft gray top-hat that was narrow at the brim and flared out at the crown like an old-time locomotive smokestack. They said nothing, just stood, tiredly, far out in the lot in the flare and shadows thrown by the kleig lights some distance away at the back entrance of the hall.

One of their number, a gray-haired gent, looking somewhat

like the real Uncle Sam, came out of the darkness and said, Fellows, the bus won't be here for another 2½ hours. Shall we wait or get back to town the best way we can?

They shuffled a moment, and, like cows leaving the pasture, started forward in the darkness. I fell in with them. Ahead of me was a huge Negro Uncle Sam, a stout, round-shouldered man, carrying his coat over one arm, his hat pushed back on his head, his left shirt-tail out. All of them walked flat-footed in weariness and silence.

What is this? I asked the nearest one.

This, he said, is the Uncle Sam Republican Club Marching Unit of Buffalo, New York. We came here on a bus to march in the demonstration. Now we are going home.

I hope we don't have to march all the way, he added.

Who's eligible to join?

Any good Republican, he said.

What's a good Republican?

Anybody who voted Republican in the last election or anybody who is going to vote Republican in the next election or anybody who likes to march and has the money to buy a uniform.

We have been marching since 1896, he said, and we have been coming to the convention since 1920.

They reached the street and scattered, getting into taxis, disappearing into the el, climbing aboard city buses, heading into restaurants, Uncle Sams going in every direction, and in a moment they were gone.

I started counting back in my mind over the convention years—1920 . . . 1924 . . . 1928 . . . 1932 . . . 1936 . . . 1940 . . . 1944 . . . 1948 . . . 1952 . . . 1956 . . . Suddenly it seemed to me that I had been at the two conventions only a matter of seconds.

---

# KINDLY CUT THAT EARTHQUAKE OUT

Every volcanic eruption on Hawaii reminds me of the earthquake that shook Pierre.

Pierre was an actor and 47. (That doesn't look nearly as old to me now.) Because of his age he was inducted into our outfit of 4-F's collected by the Army during the manpower shortage in World War II.

On Pierre's first day in the Army a sergeant asked him if he were interested in doing stagework. AM I? shouted Pierre. JUST SHOW ME! The sergeant took him to the post theater and showed him a stage on which sat a bucket of creosote suds and a scrub-brush. Do a good job, said the sergeant, and I will nominate you for an academy award.

The service was full of subtle fellows like that, and shortly after we landed on Hawaii, Pierre notified the 15 others in our barracks that he never intended to speak to anybody again as long as he was in the Army.

It's not that I don't like you fellows, he said. It's just that the the sight of you makes me sick.

Instead of gaining the peace he sought, Pierre got more attention than ever. Bets began to build on the first man who could get Pierre to speak, even if only to say hello. One afternoon I burst into the barracks and there was Pierre stretched out on his back on the old sack, his eyes closed.

Hello, Pierre, I said, just to let him know I saw him.

There was no answer. I was climbing on my own cot when suddenly a slght tremor shook the barracks, a funny sensation, as if the hide of the old earth had crawled a little bit, a mule shaking off a fly.

By George, I thought, THAT was an earthquake, and that instant there came another, stronger shudder. Out the window the landscape was all wavery, as if under water.

I glanced over at Pierre. He still lay there, eyes closed, but his face was set in grim lines and his hands were locked on the sides of his cot.

The third quake was so strong that it shook everything off the shelves over-head. I hung on to a post in the middle of the floor and looked over at Pierre on his cot where tubes, jars, and pictures of loved ones were raining all around and over him.

When the turbulence subsided, Pierre, his eyes still closed, said wearily, as if from a great distance: All right, Friddell, so I'll say hello. NOW WILL YOU KINDLY CUT THAT OUT!

# A TICKET FOR IRWIN

This is my favorite baseball story, though there's not much baseball in it. One of those present saw what happened and passed it along.

A party of Richmonders traveled to the World Series in 1952 when Brooklyn was playing the Yankees. One day, hurrying to the game, they dropped into a tiny kosher delicatessen, a hole in the wall within a homerun shot of the Brooklyn park.

The owner, an excitable little fellow, planked down crates on which they perched behind the counter as he raced around the assembling the sandwiches.

On the side he dispensed statisics of every sort on the Dodgers. His was a partisanship that Southerners could appreciate. In fact, between pastrami and statistics, they let the time get away from them and had to leave in a rush. At the doorway, one of them, Henry Dawson, looked back and yelled to the shop owner: Hurry up, Irwin.

I'm not going.

NOT GOING! Why not?

No ticket.

Dawson came back into the shop.

I haven't got an extra ticket now, he said, but I'll tell you this: IF Brooklyn wins again next year, and IF we get back up here, you-are-going-to-have-a-ticket.

With a good many, the promise would have been a gesture of the moment, forgotten in the next block, but that's not Dawson's way.

All the next year, following the fortunes of the Dodgers and the Yankees that brought them into a second successive series, Dawson had that promise in the back of his mind. When he left for New York, he had the extra ticket in his pocket.

He hadn't been able to reach Irwin because there was no phone in the shop, nor did he have Irwin's last name and address, and he had an idea that while neither rain nor snow nor dark of night could stay those couriers in the swift completion of their appointed rounds, they might be stopped cold by a letter addressed to "Irwin, Brooklyn."

This is all a waste of time, he told Bob Brenaman as they rode toward Brooklyn. Even if we find Irwin, he won't remember.

They got off the elevated and turned into into the block that held Irwin's shop, and what followed, says Brenaman, was almost like an explosion that just kept going on.

First there were children popping out of the pavement, it seemed, jiggling around the two big men, racing ahead of them down the sidewalk, screaming, He's here! He's here! He came! He came!

All along the block, says Brenaman, people were out on their steps, waving, watching, nodding in a pleased way, as if it were a great moment in which they were all taking vital roles. For that time, says Brenaman, I felt I understood Brooklyn.

Near the shop, there was a commotion at the doorway, and Irwin appeared, shaky with emotion, escorted, no, supported, by friends. He was dressed in his best, right down to new shoe laces. He was ready to go to the game.

I knew you'd come, said Irwin.

Later, at the game, the Brooks made a great play that brought everybody up cheering. Well, nearly everybody. Dawson just sat, staring out at the field. He was, Brenaman remembers, right haggard-looking.

What's the matter with you? asked Brenaman.

Suppose I'd forgotten, said Dawson.

---

# CONCERNING SENSIBLE GIFTS

In childhood Christmas meant the molasses drip of minutes while a younger brother or sister sleepily pulled on clothes. Then, suddenly, when it was time to head down the hall toward the growing glow and star-burst of the great tree, there was a panicky moment of hanging back, a reluctance to end the wonder for another 12 months. The rest of the day, while still sweet, was a gradual falling off from the first lump-in-the-throat sight of the tree, the gifts and the laughing, eye-rubbing family. (Of course, there was another wave-like rise of wonder the day after Christmas when a child examined his own and other's presents in the light of an ordinary, bearable day.)

The star-burst is still there on Christmas morning, reflected in the eyes of children everywhere, but there is an added pleasure now in the quiet 15 or 20 minutes that occur at some point during the late afternoon or evening when the house is as still as an exhausted puppy, the tree lights are more like embers than stars, the icicles criss-cross the rug in silver snail tracings, the scent of pine sap and orange peel is heavy on the air. It's a time to reflect and turn over memories, ever green and berry bright, of a minute ago or a lifetime back.

There were the special treasures socked away in the very toe of the stockings, an agate taw, a little girl's ring and the elders saying how overjoyed *they* had been on Christmas morning to find even an orange and some raisins in *their* stockings. One was over-heard telling the same story this morning to an entranced member of the third generation.

There was the rare time when the miracle of snow was joined to the miracle of Christmas and snow ice cream was added to the breakfast of steaming oyster stew. There are memories of old and absent friends held fast over the years by paper links of Christmas cards.

There are the sturdy carols that never fade even under the onslaught of radio and television. There's Crosby's "White Christmas" that tells of heavy hearts for loved ones away in two wars and the exhilarating realization that today there is no war.

There are the Christmas lights along the block, expressing the neighbors' moods, a discreet wreath with a single candle here, an exuberant out-pouring over there of light and bulbs.

There is the reassurance that on this one day at least old scores can be erased, old scars dismissed. There is a prayer for those who cannot sit at peace, but watch through the day at a bedside, or in poverty.

The other week the newspaper quoted a psychiatrist as saying that Christmas is an awful wrench on the human constitution because so many of us have to act better than we are. He was almost correct. It's not that we have to act better than we are . . . It's the fact that we don't have the means—the cash—to act as good as we'd like to. It's the strain of trying to go into debt only modestly while answering the fires of human kindness roaring in everybody's hearts.

Nor, as some hold, do I believe the season's over-commercialized. At the end of December's cold, dark corridor, the Christmas tree sheds its radiance, a last chance for everybody to fire great, swooshing Roman candles of the spirit, a mighty effort to voice the unutterable, to make things for a moment as we wish they were always. The emotional gift-giving goes back beyond Santa Claus to the three wise men. And, after all, how wisely and sensibly did THEY shop? Gold . . . frankincense . . . and myrhh . . .for a babe in a manger?

---

# JEKYLL - HYDE CONDUCTING

That was a great pops concert we put on the other day at the Richmond Arena, and I mean WE.

Up on the stage Conductor Edgar Schenkman was shaping a beguiling skein of music with his baton, and out in the bleachers, fierce as Toscanini, we parents were holding an iron hand over our children. One parent put it this way later: I didn't care if the place fell apart so long as mine were quiet.

Everybody had different methods of maintaining order. A father, quite expansive about it afterwards, said it was simple. He sat his four charges (three of his own and a neighbor's) directly in front of him, and when any one of them showed a disposition to make a noise, he reached over and thwacked the child over the hand smartly with a rolled program.

He looked like Lionel Hampton at the vibraphone. Midway through the concert, as the tension mounted, he got added authority by rolling his fountain pen into the program.

I might take up conducting, he told me modestly. Only as an avocation, you understand..

My problem was a little more subtle in nature. I couldn't reach mine. My wife sat between me and the three boys. To avoid a pitched battle in the stands, she said.

I had to rely on gestures and grimaces to hold them under my sway. At first, I kept them in order with a well-directed glare, but as Conductor Schenkman's pace picked up, so did mine. I would hold my hand high, and bring the right against it in a sharp, spanking motion, or chop the air with the left hand and do a rapid twirl with the right fingers, as if cutting off a television set for a week. At one point, I simply grabbed my neck with both hands, rolled my eyes, and stuck out my tongue.

You should have seen me during "The Ride of the Valkyries." One woman, sitting in the next section, did. She said it looked like Lon Chaney changing Dr. Jekyll into Mr. Hyde.

At intermission, when the rest of the audience thronged around the drink stands, I took my three out into the parking lot and we put on a scale version of the Olympic games—the 100-yard dash, leap the chain, push-ups, tag, run around the Arena, and help Guybo get up off the ground.

The audience in the Arena was as quiet as any I ever heard in a concert hall. There was even less coughing from nervous adults. We were too busy conducting to cough.

Going out, parents, children in tow, said to one another, beaming: They did splendidly, didn't they?

They could have been talking about the musicians, the children, or both.

---

# ELEPHANTS DRINKING

They stood swaying, six great pyramids against the flat, blue sky. Even the sun looked small.

There were three men in white coveralls and a knot of boys watching, and the knot had a way of backing off as one or another of the elephants shifted his big bulk. Everyone was silent, even the handlers, watching elephants drink water out in the open, on the plain of the State Fair grounds.

There was a truck pumping water unendingly into a bright new GI can, and the elephants, their big heads together, drew it out just as steadily. A thirsty elephant would curl his trunk in his mouth and seem to say Ah-h-h-h-h for almost a minute and then poke the trunk back in the water.

Occasionally one of them would sweep water across his dusty knees or toss a great snoutful, geyser-like, over his broad back. Then it would stream down his sides for a long time, like water running off a big boulder at the sea's edge when the tide retreats.

There was a sound of surf, too, in the drinking.

One of the boys edged forward and, stuttering a little, asked how much that elephant would drink, meaning any one or all six, or just anything he could learn about elephants. The white-clad handler didn't turn his head. The boy fell back but in a minute moved over to a red-faced man at the truck's pump.

"How much—" began the boy.

"On a hot day," said the man, "400 gallons."

They watched the elephants, sad-eyed and happy, drink some more.

"On a very hot day, all day," the man said, drawing his breath, "500 gallons."

One of the elephants, satisfied, put his big head, horse-like, close to his handler's.

"On a hot day in August," said the man, thinking, "I've had to stand at this here pump for an hour . . . or more."

The elephants shambled across the lot, dark wet splashes on their yellowish gray hides, a great gray moving mountain range of elephants.

"On a hot day," the boy told his companions as they started toward the high shining white hill of the Big Top, "on a hot day, maybe a thousand gallons."

---

# DOGS, CATS, AND POLITICS

Driving home from a party, my wife asks: 1. Why were you so silent, so stick-like all evening? or, 2. What on earth got into you that you talked so much?

She's right, too. There's never a happy medium.

Last night was one of the talkative ones. I opened by remarking, mildly, that the election was pretty nearly a split because all the cat lovers had voted for Nixon and all the dog lovers had backed

Kennedy. It turned out that a majority in the room were dog lovers who had voted for Nixon, and I got nowhere with the defense that they, subconsciously, REALLY preferred cats.

You KNOW you do, I shouted, Admit it! Admit it! Be honest for once.

They got quite beastly about it.

Surviving that, I chanced to mention that the wives of all four candidates—Mesdames Nixon, Kennedy, Lodge, and Johnson—should have stayed home and not gone traipsing about the country campaigning. To my astonishment the whole question changed to the point that presently I was arguing that ALL wives should stay at home, something I would never assert in a calmer moment.

All the time, nervously, I was devouring a dish of ripe olives at my elbow. Something I have always meant to ask my wife is what do you do with olive pits in polite company? You can't cross the room in front of everybody and drop them clunk, clunk, clunk into an ash tray; and it seems so, I don't know . . . crass somehow to spit them on the floor.

There I was arguing an indefensible position with 14 olive pits in my mouth. At one point, leaning over to pound the floor for emphasis, I swallowed at least seven pits and pitched right over on my face with a high, strangling whoop, like a dying Indian on Wagon Train. It put an end to THAT topic, anyway.

Honestly, said my wife, as we drove home, What possessed you to dive out into the floor like that?

It was those confounded olive pits, I told her.

---

# DEBATE — AND VOTE

A tired-looking friend explained this morning he had a political hangover. The strange thing was, that he had nothing to drink at the party, not even a glass of water.

He was taking off his coat, when his host asked casually how he saw the election, and my friend said casually he was thinking about voting for Nixon.

That was the last complete sentence he uttered all evening. Kennedy supporters rushed over and surrounded him so that, he said, he felt as if he were back in childhood playing bull in the ring, and he was "it".

(Before we get any futher in this incident, let's note that the target would change from place to place. In another setting, for instance, the man in the center could be a Kennedy supporter. The point is, that ANY of us could wind up in the center, and probably has.)

An intense housewife, hands on hips, face within a foot of his, would talk at him steadily for 10 minutes until she had to pause and take a breath.

Yes, but—he would say, and at that she would drift off, and he would find himself facing a totally new and fresh adversary, already talking full steam. At a quarter of two, when he turned to go, he had been on his feet all evening and found he hadn't moved six feet from the front door.

It may not be the most interesting election in this century, but it's certainly the most discussed.

Another friend told me he followed an argument over crop subsidies between two farmers in a store out on Route 6 that beat anything he ever heard for pure volume. At the height of it, a young fellow sitting on the side said, Say, who are you fellows for?

They paused to check, impatiently, and the argument ended, eerily. They were for the same man.

Another funny thing is that nobody wants to talk about his own candidate . . . just attack the other, as if neither could bear to LOOK at his own man's shortcomings for fear, I guess, that he might not get to the polls at all.

This negative approach is in contrast to the election, say, of 1952, when you were very much FOR Ike, the national hero who could grin away our troubles without much effort on our part, or for Adlai, the sparkling phrase-maker, who broke onto the scene like a fresh egg dropped sunny-side-up into a skillet.

Amid all the negative charges back and forth, there's a very small school of voters that believes that whichever is elected— Nixon or Kennedy—he has positive qualities and will prove a far better President than the opposition expects.

Thinking back, over the miles they have traveled, the range of topics they have touched, their cool courage under the fire of television bouts, I'm proud of both—and the country that produced them.

But don't let me stop you.
You go ahead and argue.
And vote.

---

## KENNEDY DROPS IN

The President flew across the way yesterday from his Glen Ora estate to see his Berryville neighbor—and oft-time foe— United State Senator Harry Byrd. Two helicopters landed in a little open expanse on the dogwood lawn sloping below white-pillared "Rosemont," and Byrd trudged down to meet the President as 100 guests lined the veranda to watch.

The visit had been in the making more than 10 days. A helicopter had flown over to make practice passes at the lawn, but the President's visit surprised most of the guests—senators and government officials, neighbors, and newspapermen. To one, who expressed amazement Kennedy observed, "Oh, I used to come here as a senator."

Ordinary mortals tend to look washed-out alongside the deeply-tanned President, but Byrd, as he gets older, gets ruddier. Time has whitened the fringe of hair around the rosy face with its intense blue eyes, so that there's an appearance of frosty, crackling energy about him.

The President, tall, slightly hunched, as if about to take off on an end run in a touch football game, moved among the guests, not just greeting them, but trying in a matter of seconds to establish a contact with each, strike up a discussion, ring an idea into the conversation.

To Samuel Bemiss, Richmond history addict, Kennedy observed that a helicopter was ideal from which to study Stonewall Jackson's Valley campaign, and with that the two of them began talking about the Civil War, winding up with Bemiss observing how much he regretted seeing the current centennial tend to lose its way in over-commercialization and the re-enactment of battles. The President said he agreed. Two hours later, leaving, the President startled Bemiss by bidding him goodby by name and saying how much he had enjoyed the talk on Jackson.

One eddy brought the President into conversation with Miss Priscilla Eaves, 17, from St. Timothy's near Baltimore. It turned out, under the President's questioning that she was bent on entering Smith, she hoped. "Oh, you'll get in," the President reassured her

He engaged in a deep discussion with Mortimer Caplin, Charlottesville professor who became commissioner of internal revenue. Caplin remarked how much the tax department employees had enjoyed a surprise visit by Kennedy last week. It was the first time he said, that a President had ever just walked in that way to say hello.

Caplin said he had started to write the President a note of thanks, but had decided that going through channels the note would lose its effervescence. You should have written me directly, said the President who makes a habit of disregarding channels.

The guests wound past a buffet in the dining room and then took seats at card tables placed in the two large front parlors, the huge entrance hall, and a side porch. The wives of two of Byrd's boys, Mrs. Harry Byrd Jr. and Mrs. Richard Byrd, took the President to the head of a huge oval table in the dining room.

Byrd's Spring luncheon parties move with an easy elegance, but there's also the informal note of a family reunion among the members of that close-knit club, the United State Senate. The seats around the big oval table fill as casually as those at the cards tables, except that yesterday there was a tendency to hang back at taking a seat at the President's table.

I was last in line, a sort of caboose, and moving out of the dining room, my efforts focused at trying not to trip and toss a plateful of cole slaw and Smithfield ham through the air in the presence of the President of the United States, I heard Mrs. Harry Byrd Jr. calling to me from the head of the table to take the last seat. Around the end on my left, were three senators and their wives: Clinton P. Anderson of New Mexico, Lister Hill of Alabama, and Eugene McCarthy of Minnesota. On my right was pretty Miss Eaves, whom the President had decided was going to be admitted to Smith College.

Her presence prompted the President to observe what a pity it was that intelligent young girls failed to use their college education more directly and become doctors, lawyers, and scientists.

The two Byrd wives took up a defense of motherhood, and the President puffed on a cigar and kept them going with questions, more out of a desire, it seemed, to draw out their ideas than express a committed view of his own. At one point he inquired whether the placing of children in nursery schools, as is often done in Europe, hurt them scholastically or emotionally. When the two ladies caught him in a cross-fire of objections, he observed, laughing, that women seemed to resent efforts to raise their status.

Then he looked down the table and asked Miss Eaves what she intended to do when she got out of college. Miss Eaves said she would decide after she got IN college. Ask him, I murmured to her, whether he thinks Mrs. Jacqueline Kennedy should go back to work as an inquiring newspaper reporter.

Miss Eaves, re-phrasing the question beautifully, called, "Mr. President . . . After a woman has married, should she go back to her job?"

Kennedy broke out laughing, and said it might be a good idea, but perhaps it wouldn't be wise for him to generalize.

Byrd, who limps slightly from a fall on the ice in 1950, moved from room to room, an old bear who caught his foot in a trap once and isn't likely to do so again. Senator Anderson, who has fought with and against Byrd many times, regarded him fondly, murmuring: Harry Byrd is a wonderfully warm man. Treat him with kindness and he responds (raising again the image of the old bear.) At heart, said Anderson, "Harry Byrd is a sentimentalist."

This brought to my mind a time when Byrd said, with clinical detachment, as if the matter were quite out of his hands: "Some who were once my friends are now my enemies and some who used to be my enemies are now my friends."

But Anderson beamed at the sight of the young President and old Byrd breaking bread. "The President knows," he said, "that Harry Byrd has a place in the Senate. Break it down and every senator has a reason for being there. This President would never do, as Truman did, and say there were too many Byrds in the Senate. I'm not being critical of Truman. It's just that they do things a little differently."

This day boded well for Kennedy's program in Congress,

decided Anderson, and, as Byrd was clumping by, the senator from New Mexico grabbed his hand, leaned back, and said, "Harry, this coudn't have happened to two nicer person."

Byrd only laughed, clapped him on the shoulder, and moved on.

As the President was departing down the center hall, the Negro servants came to get his autograph. The President moved on to the veranda, and down the steps, murmuring his thanks. Byrd stumped along at his side, affable as ever . . . and unchanged, too when he would take his seat in the Senate Monday.

The guests lined the veranda again, watching the two move away in the dogwood, one senator remarking to another, "Well now THAT was exciting, wasn't it."

A Secret Service man came hurrying from the house, pushing his way through the crowd, carrying something.

Anderson explained, "The President forgot his hat."

---

# SOUNDS FOR A FALLOUT SHELTER

To lighten long hours underground, a psychologist suggests we equip fallout shelters with tape recordings of the ordinary sounds of the world outside. Much as Noah got together a zoo, I guess.

A soothing sound, says the psychologist, would be that of a refrigerator stopping and starting.

Whose refrigerator?

Not ours.

It starts with a whining clunk and a great shuttering roar as if the whole house has cut its moorings and is putting out to sea. At that racket friends visiting us for the first time have started up, a wild light in their eyes, and shouted, We're moving!

There will be no reverberating refrigerator in my survival shelter, but there might be these, or something like them.

Since there would be no night, no day, when it came time to sleep, I'd turn on the country sound of acres of crickets, katydids, and cicadas sawing away in the night, a dry symphony running up and down the scale. It would recall the calm of a rural front porch where the adults, after a hard day, rock and listen, and the children, half-lulled, half-irritated, are always on the point of getting up and finding something to do, yet wanting to stay, too, and try to pin down the choruses. This one stitches loud and close, and when that batch ceases for a moment, another section chimes in from way down in the meadow, alway sounding, never ceasing, an endless tuning up, now near, now far, shifting tapestries of sound, laminated lamentations of a thousand thousand night-criers.

For the hours of the day there would be bird calls: at dawn a cardinal's steadily stropping whistle, rising on the morning air, at noon a crow talking lazily in the top of a pine, at dusk, the quiet-paced benediction of a wood thrush.

I'd take along the sound of children running along a hard-packed beach at the edge of a crashing surf . . . the muffled flumping of a dog bounding through fresh snow . . . a collie lapping water unendingly on a hot day . . . a chain of children roller-skating down a hill in swooping curves and loops and loops of laughter.

I'd like the comfortable sound of someone opening the evening paper, turning it leisurely page by page, clearing his throat and chuckling once or twice, the sound of it enough to bring back the whole scene mellow in the lamplight . . . someone preparing breakfast quietly in the early morning as you awaken slowly . . . or cutting roses in the garden . . . the liquid patter of hundreds of feet hurrying along a street.

I'd want a river of wind rushing through the trees . . . the snare-drumming of an advancing wall of rain as it comes slowly across the landscape and breaks with a many-fisted roar on your roof . . . a thunderstorm cracking a blinding whip through the night skies . . . And finally, the moving, rocking ocean rhythms of a Sunday morning congregation singing Rock of Ages.

There are some of mine, and, gentle readers, wherever you are, what are yours?

For colors in the survival shelter the psychologist suggests blue on the ceiling, green on the walls, and an earthy beige underfoot —a scheme, he notes with scientific detachment, that "would help the occupants remember which way was up."

Also, let's add, the colors recall the beloved outside world.

It would test man's resources, the psychologist warns.

Noah took it for 40 days. I guess we could stand it for 14.

But no refrigerators, please.

# "WAR AND PEACE" AT SEA

This is a valentine for my library friends, patient and enduring. Not a week passes but what they don't rescue me with a fact or a book that I could never locate.

I take out books like other peaple resort to aspirin. It's wonderfully restoring to walk into the house with an armload of books and fling them across the floor (but gently, of course), calling to the family to come and see. In school one day, different children were saying that their fathers could do this and that of a prodigious nature and, after a time, one of mine offered: Guybo sure can bring home library books.

Generally, I keep about 30 rotating between home and the Richmond Public Library, the Belmont branch, and the State Library. On lean days when the fines outrun the cash in my pocket, the librarians keep a sort of informal charge account. On flush days, clearing the slate, I add a dollar or two for future fines.

Our most difficult time came during the war.

I was meeting and trying the saintly patience of the new librarians all across the country. The book that gave us the most trouble was "War and Peace." I'd get along 183 pages into that book, and then the outfit would get orders to depart pronto for a new camp, and I'd return the book.

At the next camp, I'd check out another copy of "War and Peace" and start all over from page one. The book is so infernally complex that it pretty nearly has to be read at one sitting, or you lose all count of the characters.

Turn out for KP, Friddell, Sergeant Maypop would call.

Don't bother me, I said. I'm reading "War and Peace."

I'll read 'till you get back and tell you what happened, he said. NOW GET OUT OF HERE!

Four times I returned "War and Peace" without finishing it. The fifth place was Oahu, Hawaii, from which our outfit embarked on a 42-day voyage, so hastily, that I couldn't return the book.

It was just as well. There was almost nothing to read aboard ship, and three dozen of us read "War and Peace" simultaneously.

We did it by tearing off the cover, dividing the book into its neat, sewn sections, and passing them out in order. As one man finished a section, he would hand it to the next in line and go look for the section due him, standing guard at a discreet distance to see that nothing happened to his portion. We read "War and Peace" to pieces.

---

# PARTY POOPER

Ever so often at a party somebody says: Oh, let's play Charades . . . or 20 Questions . . . or Categories.

That's when I know how Custer felt at the Little Big Horn.

I haven't been able to hold my own in a party game since Drop the Hankchef in 1927.

I would just as soon make out an income tax, or go back to school.

To me, there's little difference in answering questions in school and somebody's living room, except that you do not have to sit on the floor in school.

It's doubly hard answering questions at a party because to save wear on my good suit, I'm trying to sit lightly on the rug, trying, in fact, to float a couple of inches ABOVE the rug, like an Indian Yoga.

Even when you don't think, there's something oppressive about being in a room where everybody else is thinking. The air is heavy with thought patterns and you hesitate to clear your throat.

I never even surmount the first obstacle, the explanation by the hostess of rules roughly equivalent to the theory of relativity.

Just fly by the seat of your pants, I tell myself, and remember that Coleridge said: The saints will aid if men will call, For the blue sky bends over all.

One of the toughest games is Numbers where everybody sits in a circle, and I can't tell you anything more about it from that point on.

All I know is there's lots of calling of numbers around the circle and clapping when you hit a certain number or its multiple, and then the game reaches me—and stops.

All right, we were going good there for a minute, says the hostess, until we hit Friddell. Let's try again.

The counting and clapping start again, pick up speed amid a lot of hilarity, and then suddenly everybody is looking at me in cold silence, and I can't remember what number comes after 9.

Give him a hint somebody, calls the hostess.

How about cat on a hot WHAT roof? suggests the fellow to my left.

TAR! I shout. I've got it! Nine, TAR.

Even worse than Numbers are games where they cook up some riddle or skit while you're not present and then call you in and watch you, a silent circle of wolves around a lame ptarmingan.

There's always the thought, too, that after they send me out of the room, they all may adjourn quickly to some other house. It's happened.

----

# BARING THE SOLE

In the paper the other day a fellow, a shoe salesman, said every man should own at least 30 pairs of shoes. (The average woman already has that many, or so it seems when you're looking through the closet for your extra pair.)

He said doctors made Mr. Eisenhower change his shoes three times a day. I go Ike one better and take OFF my shoes at every opportunity, particularly when grappling with a heavy problem.

My guess is that the blood, in swinging around the body, is not slowed down when there are no constricting shoes at the south turn, and so the head gets fresh blood faster, which makes for clearer thinking. I have not checked the AMA on this theory. Maybe I'm wrong. Maybe my brains are in my feet.

Anyway, in an emergency, off come the old shoes.

The day I lost my first job, management called me in and said, gracefully, Friddell, you're fired.

Hold it, I said, let's take off our shoes and talk this thing over.

You're fired again, he roared.

Going barefoot, come June 1, used to be a custom widely followed in my youth. Barefoot Day was as big, in its way, as Christmas morning. It came near school closing, and when you shucked your shoes it was as if you were kicking off all the world's cares. It symbolized Summer freedom, a day of gladiation. When you sprang out the back door and leaped across the green grass barefoot, it was as if you could bound over trees. There was a new world of caressing texture underfoot, the soft silt of dust sifting between your toes, the cool, sucking glut of mud, the tender pad of grass, the rough, springy mat of a forest floor, the cold sweep of a creek.

I believe it would lend a note of laughable informality around here if we all went barefoot.

All of us, I mean.

You, me and the whole city barefoot.

Bankers, policeman, school teachers, housewives and newspapermen.

Even politicians.

It's impossible to be pompous barefoot. Your feet give you away. It's impossible to make a resounding speech barefooted. Nobody would take you seriously. You'd have to stick to the bare facts or you'd lose your audience in hilarity. All politicians should make speeches while they are standing barefooted on a gravel driveway. Or on a hot tar road.

It's impossible to make absurd demands barefooted. Can you picture a barefoot summit conference?

Are you—ha, ha—asking for West Berlin in your—ho, ho—bare feet? Mr. Kennedy would ask.

Well, yes, but—ho, ho, ho—thinking it over in my—ha, ha bare feet, the whole thing looks ridiculous, Khrushchev would say. Let's go wade some place.

All the idea needs is a nudge.

Begin here and the craze will spread like crabgrass. We would become known as the barefoot city. Tourists would come miles to see us. And we could sell them our old shoes.

Barefoot people of Richmond, arise!

Throw off your laces!

You have nothing to lose but your shoes.

# PLAYING THE GAME

Barrels of fun! said the signs. Any two or four can play!

It looked like an ideal gift for a boy's birthday, a hockey game on a board as big bath mat with 12 little tin players that swung sticks and whacked around a marble when maneuvered by levers at each end of the board.

I checked to see that there were no electric motors or atomic reactors tied in with the thing. It's getting so a man can't play with his own children unless he has a degree in nuclear physics. Nothing difficult here, I thought. Easy as pie.

Wrap it up, I said, but the clerk, smiling, reached under the counter and handed me an unopened box.

A man may smile and smile and be a villain.

That night, after the boy was abed, I opened the box, and found a bare board and scads of separate little tissue-wrapped pieces, dibs and dabs of this and that, and a scroll of directions that would choke King Tut.

Honey, I called, PUT ON THE COFFEE and get Wernher von Braun on the phone. I've got to mantle this game.

An hour later, flat on my back and the game suspended across two dining-room chairs above me, I was working away when my wife's father dropped in, the weekly inspection he makes at my house to see that nobody is starving. He picked up the directions. Easy as pie, he said.

He began to read them in an extra loud voice, as if sheer sound would impart sense, as if volume would lend enlightenment. By midnight, working on shifts under the dining room chairs, we got the game together. Make sure it works, he suggested. Play you a game.

We got on our knees at each end of the board, and one of his men got the marble and I was swinging my men in line to block his shot when he shouted WAIT A MINUTE! WAIT A MINUTE!

I looked up in alarm, thinking he had a stitch in his side and WHAM he shot the marble into the net at my end of the board.

The game went along briskly, neither of us getting a clear shot until suddenly he shouted again, HOLD IT! HOLD IT! leaned across the board as if to straighten one of the players with his left hand, and when I settled back on my knees to watch, rammed home another goal with his right hand. For the first time I caught the full force of that old saying about it matters not whether you win or lose, IT'S HOW YOU PLAY THE GAME.

I slid a pencil under the board at my end, and won steadily for five minutes, and then he began winning, unaccountably, until I saw he had a book under his end.

When I won the first game, he shouted, TWO OUT OF THREE ! TWO OUT OF THREE ! and when I won the third game, he insisted, FOUR OUT OF SEVEN! FOUR OUT OF SEVEN!

At 3 a.m. he announced, triumphantly, FIFTY-ONE OUT OF ONE HUNDRED! My game! My series! Time to quit!

Don't sulk, he added. A man's got to learn to be a good loser.

I helped direct him out of the driveway, resisting the temptation to guide him in the ditch, and then, weaving from weariness and hockey knees, I slipped into the boy's room and placed the game at the foot of his bed, quietly, I thought. Then I dove into bed and slumber. At 3:10 a.m. I was awakened by a gentle but persistent shaking at my shoulder, and a voice, just turning 6 years old, at my ear saying quietly but firmly, Get up, Guybo, get up. Let's play hockey.

Some days you just can't win.

---

# TOP BANANA AT THE MET

Soon the Richmond Symphony will be holding its first concert of the season, and I wouldn't miss it for a jar of lightning bugs.

General Meyer, the president, checks with me after every concert to see how much I was able to understand. You see, he explained one day, if we reach you, Friddell, we can reach ANYBODY.

My efforts at a musical education began 14 years ago with a

visit to the Metropolitan Opera Company in New York. (My
wife and I run up to New York to catch the best plays at LEAST
once every 15 years. I am hoping next year we can make it to
"Oklahoma!" if all goes well.)

On the 1947 trip we were tooling along in a taxi when she
said, Oh, how I would love to see the Met.

Your wish is my command, I told her. Whip over to the Met,
ole top, I told the driver.

The taxi drew up alongside a big barn of a building, and I
said, THERE . . . you've seen the Met. Now head for the Bronx
Zoo and the elephants, ole sport!

But I wanted to see INSIDE, she wailed.

YOU MEAN YOU WANT TO GO IN THAT PLACE, I
yelled, appalled.

For shame, said the driver, Take her in, Diamond Jim.

On the way, I tried to snag a copy of The Daily News but
concluded from the look on her face that you cannot read a tabloid
at the Met, only the New York Times or the Herald Tribune.

Inside, there's the stage, long enough for a track meet, and, out
front of the stage, a huge semicircle of seats, tier on tier, reaching
up a dozen decks, until the people in the topmost circle hang directly
overhead, like bananas on a stalk.

It reminded me of the old-time beehive, built up in rings with
golden walls of wax, and at each level of the hive, people were
pouring in, brilliant bees, humming, flashing jeweled wings. It was
a little, too, like standing in the midst of a blazing, revolving
chandelier.

I looked up, up, to the last seat at the end of the topmost ring,
which I sensed more than saw up there in the gloom, smack over
against the wall to the side of the stage.

Boy! I said. The poor soul that sits there is going to need a
seat belt and a telescope. Well, let's go.

We kept climbing, deck after deck, until I felt like bawling
Excelsior! to those we passed, until at last we reached the top deck
and the last two seats, smack against the wall, the very perch to
which I had pointed a scant 45 minutes before.

It was a memorable experience. I couldn't go to sleep for fear
I'd lose my grip and come spraddling down out of the sky onto
the stage, an impromptu deus ex machina. Once or twice a soldier

in the opera, a guard, would step too near the footlights, and we could just catch a glimpse of the top of his hat. To this day my wife refers to Aida as "The Guard's Hat." I remember it was Aida because midway through, trying to keep my mind off the height, I discovered that Aida spelled the same backwards as forwards.

Or does it?

---

# EVER SINCE EVE

There was a note in my typewniter: Your wife called and says be sure and bring home grout.

I did not know what grout was and had a hunch nobody else would either.

Women have been sending men on cryptic missions like that ever since Eve.

I dropped into a delicatessen and asked, casually, for a half pound of grout.

Kraut? said the clerk.

Grout.

Trout?

Grout.

We're all out of grout, he said, firmly.

When do you expect to have any? I asked.

Never, he said.

In a department store I asked a fellow in men's wear: Sir, where should I go for grout?

I'd suggest you go to a doctor quickly as possible, he said.

Madam, I said to a lady in notions, Will you PLEASE tell me the way to grout?

Certainly, she said, you go out simply by walking through that door six feet from where you're standing.

It was like running an obstacle course in the army, but at last I found the grout, a can of the stickiest-looking glue I'd ever seen.

Okay, I said, phoning home, I've got the grout.   Anything else?

Yes, she said.   Please bring me 39 green tiles.

Towels?   I asked.

Tiles, she said.

Look, Honey, I said.   Your Southern accent is deepening so much it's even hard for ME to understand.   Did you say towels?

YOU'RE talking more like a Yankee every day, she said.   I want 39 TILES.

All right, I said.   I'll get 39 towels, but there's such a thing as putting cleanliness BEFORE godliness.

At home I found her gluing tiny green TILES on a plywood board for a coffee table.

Don't worry, she told me.   I can fix these towels for Christmas presents.   Just run down to the store and get me some rick rack.

---

# WHO LET THAT COW IN HERE?

I don't even like educational TV anymore.

Most people, martyrs to the cause, insist that it's only because of the educational programs that they put up with the other.

Not me and Robert Hatcher.

We are putting up with the educational TV.

For weeks, Hatcher told me the other day, he has been going out to get the paper at 6:30 every morning and there, on the TV screen, is a guy at a blackboard talking about advanced calculus, thermodynamics, or something else so abstruse that it makes the theory of relativity seem child's play.

At 6:30 IN THE MORN-ING! said Hatcher.

It struck me as monstrous, too, but I didn't know just how monstrous until I got home late Friday night from covering the Inaugural of the bouffant hairdo.

Don't wake me in the morning, I told my wife.   The strain of seeing hundreds of thousands of Jackie Kennedy hairdos has undone me.

She promised, but she should have put a stakeout around me, as they say on TV, because while she was puttering around the kitchen, as women WILL do, and I was deep in sleep, the oldest boy came at 6:30 a.m. and stood by my ear.

Guybo, he said, softly, insistently, Gnybo, there's a man on TV talking about a cow with a window in its stomach.

I came awake fast.

IN THIS ROOM, I shouted, A COW? AT THIS HOUR OF THE MORNING? WHO LET HIM IN?

Not in HERE, he said. It's on TV. The man says the cow has a window in its stomach.

Your're kidding, I said, sinking back on the pillow. Why should they do a thing like that to a cow?

To see what's going on in its stomach. To study the roughage.

Fascinating, I said. Go catch some more and tell your mother while ole Guybo thinks it over.

He left the room, and I plunged back into sleep. In about five seconds, it seemed, there was another voice at my ear, the middle boy this time.

Guybo, he said, do you know what they call a cow's stomach?

No, I said, Nobody ever told me.

It's a RU-men, he said, trumphantly.

Then he was gone. Had it all been a dream, by George?

It wasn't because in another five minutes there was another voice, the five-year-old's.

Guess how many stomachs a cow has? he whispered in my ear.

How many? I asked. I give up.

And I meant it.

---

# KILROY WAS THERE

I saw Kilroy.

. . . Before he became a myth, before his fame skipped across the Pacific to the United States. You remember Kilroy.

His name was everywhere toward the end of World War II —scrawled on the dusty tail-gate of a trailer-truck rumbling along Route 1, stenciled on the nose of a Guam-based bomber taking off for the Ryukyus, chalked on a subway wall in the Bronx, daubed in straggly pitch on a freight car that lay on a siding in the Georgia pinelands. Wherever you saw it, it read: "Kilroy was here."

Kilroy's calling card became a password among GI's, an ironic testament that packed war's frustrations—and triumphs—in three wry words.

Whatever it meant, I saw the myth in the making, the human Moby Dick who was everywhere before anybody else. I saw him, when the Marines were returning from Tarawa to a so-called rest camp on the Big Island of Hawaii. It was really a staging area for their next thrust into the ring of Japanese defenses.

When they landed at Hilo, they were whisked to the remote camp in every possible vehicle, including a gasoline bus-on-rails, with a couple of ancient train cars attached. This Toonerville trolley chugged around the steep cliffs, a scribble against the great green flank of the island.

It stuttered across shaky, stilt-like viaducts, lush green heights of cane on one side of the cars, and, on the other, far below, the ocean edges with natives bathing. Every bend or so, the train stopped to take on a side of beef, a bushel basket of orchids— or wait on a tourist that wanted to take its picture.

I was sitting on the back car when the Marines piled on in Hilo. Nothing I had seen impressed me as much as these men. The island was a silent backdrop as the dinky train chugged along, swaying, with its boisterous company.

At one bend an unexpected sight silenced them, a lone passenger waiting at the side of the tracks for the return trip, the prettiest girl, undoubtedly in the Pacific, tall, beautiful, in a summer yellow frock, poised smiling in the sunshine against the green Hawaiian hillside, a full-lipped smile that made the Mona Lisa a drudge. To us, she seemed barely to touch the earth.

The train coughed to a stop just around the bend, out of sight of the girl. Someone, leaning out, saw the straw-hatted driver puttering with the engine. Then, running down the side of the train came a Marine, ugly as the girl had been beautiful, his fist filled with a bunch of weedy blossoms. He was short, wiry, with dancing slate-gray eyes, and an impish grin that split his square freckled face. "That's Kilroy," said the Marine beside me.

"Who's Kilroy?"

"Kilroy," said the Marine, "has been everywhere and done

everything—to hear him. Trouble is, every time we think we've pinned him down in a lie, he comes up with just enough proof to make you think maybe Kilroy was there. When nothing else can," he added, "Kilroy can make you laugh."

There was furious betting on whether Kilroy would win any notice from the girl. One man swore she was so beautiful, she couldn't exist. She was, he insisted, a mass hallucination. If she did exist, he added, she wouldn't look at Kilroy. Half the car said she would, half said she wouldn't, and it appeared the sides continually changed.

The driver finished puttering and warmed up the engine. Our eyes were fixed on the bend. Kilroy's sitting around there trying to think up a story, murmured someone. The train began to move, and then, around the bend, Kilroy came running. A cheer ran the length of the cars, for, as they pulled him aboard, his face, I saw, was smeared from ear to ear with lipstick.

One of two things happened around that bend. Fast-talking Kilroy borrowed the girl's lipstick and smeared his freckled face, or, bemused by the dancing gray-eyed figure, the beautiful stranger really kissed him.

With Kilroy you just never knew.

I hope it was the latter.

---

# CHICKEN IN A CAVE

It being a lovey, sunsplashed day and there being lots to do around the yard, I said, Let's go to the Luray Caverns.

You know you haven't cut the grass in three weeks, said my wife, gently.

I have NEVER been to the Luray Caverns, I said. Suddenly it seems a shocking thing for a man to reach middle age and never see a cave except one he dug himself three feet in the side of a railroad cut.

That's enough, she said. Let's go.

Back in 1878 two men were walking through the woods when one felt a draught on his leg, looked down, and there was a hole

in the ground, the start of the cave and a great commercial enterprise. Getting in is a good deal more complicated now. The hole
is nowhere in sight because a rambling gift shop of field-stone, club-
house style, has been built over it. At the rear—near the Indian-
bead belts and the paperweights—is a doorway through which you
descend rather much as if going down to fire the furnace.

In the first great cave chamber, a dozen or so of us clustered
around a teen-age guide. It was a little like standing inside a well-
lit giant's mouth in need of a lot dental work.

Ladies and gentlemen, said the guide, we will start through
yonder corridor and should return through that other one in about
an hour and 10 minutes with a little luck.

Honey, I said, you and the boys go on. I shall stay here near
the entrance and observe the people who are fool enough to pay
to go underground on a day like this.

You're chicken, she said.

Precisely, I said.

For shame, she said. The boys are watching you.

Then they can stay here, too, I said, by the old cellar stairs.
Go by yourself and bring us back a full report.

I'll not stir a step without you, she said.

Pulled by her and pushed by the three boys, I started quaking
down a long throat-like corridor with red sides. The great slabs of
rock shelving on each other, now close, now far, put me in mind
of those tight places that fold in on you in dreams. Occasionally,
below or above, we would see other parties marching along single-
file like something out of Dante.

Stalactites hung down, like huge hands of tobacco, I told her.

More like crystal chandeliers, she said.

Notice the stalactites, said the guide, hanging around us like
crystal chandeliers.

At one spot we looked out on a basin of water reflecting the
spires and minarets of the ceiling, a delicate, sloping skyline from
fairyland, I murmured to her.

A burned-over forest, she whispered.

To your right, said the guide, see the ceiling reflected in water
as a burned-over forest.

In one chamber hung a stalactite in thin folds of a tan hue,
streaked red like bacon, I said.

More like a folded Indian blanket, she said.

Dead ahead, said the guide, notice the Indian-blanket stalactite.

High up on a boulder, picked out by a spotlight, was a lovely cone-shaped stalagmite shining like the Capitol dome at night, I suggested.

Or a silver Christmas tree, she said.

Look up, said the guide, and see the silver Christmas tree, table-size.

I gave up.

Near the close was a pool, a wishing well, into which each of us threw a penny, piously.  Outside, in the bright sun, I asked what they had wished for.

A birthday cake, said the 5-year-old.

A black horse with a white mane, said the 9-year-old

I'm not going to tell you because it wouldn't come true, said the 7-year-old, sensibly, like his mother.

-----

# EXCELSIOR! EXCELSIOR!

Our boys' grandmother— the one from the eccentric side of the family—will be giving them an Easter Egg hunt in mid-August, put off since April what with one thing or another.  She has been doling out candy eggs, impulsively, from the sideboard for four months, so that the August hunt will be for bubble gum with baseball cards.

It beats me how people go through life in such helter skelter fashion.  With me it is plan, plan, plan, and use the old noodle all the way.  Look how I handled last Easter.

The middle boy, the 7-year-old, said earnestly as his mother was closing his bedroom door on Easter Eve not to forget to leave out the baskets for the rabbit, the first clear indication he had decided to cast his lot this year with his guileless 5-year-old brother rather than the poker-faced 10-year-old.

About midnight I crawled around the attic, searching out the baskets and bumping my noggin on the rafters, but there was no green excelsior grass where my wife rememberd leaving it.

I bolted around to all-night drug stores bawling Excelsior?

like the man in the poem, but the first stores had only yellow or pink excelsior, an abomination, and the later ones didn't have even that, nor did the first stops on the second circuit.

Weren't you in here earlier looking for GREEN grass, asked one druggist.

Back home when I first cut loose with the old power mower in the front yard somebody raised a window down the way and bellowed in a most unrefined manner: WHAT'S GOING ON OUT THERE AT THIS HOUR?

I'm too much of a Southern gentleman to engage in a cross-fire of that sort, and so when the fellow yelled what nut was out there mowing grass at 2 a.m. on Easter morning, I yelled back, The Easter Bunny! and just let it go at that. It does no good to argue with such people.

I gathered a great pile of grass, carried it inside, lined the baskets, and then went, as the sky was lighting, to bed.

What was all that uproar out there a moment ago? asked my wife, sleepily.

Some fool down the street was making a lot of noise. I told her.

Was it the same one running a power mower? she asked.

My head had just dropped on the pillow, it seemed, when the 7-year-old was shaking my shoulder saying: Guybo, whaddaya think? The Easter rabbit left the eggs in REAL grass this year.

See what I mean? Planning.

## OLD HYMNS, OLD FRIENDS

Recently it dawned on me how difficult it was becoming to sing in church. I couldn't seem to come to grips with the tune or the words. The hymn just never settled down into any recognizable track, and when the congregation finished and sat down, I was left with the feeling of the one that had gone astray from the ninety and nine. Hymns didn't used to be this hard to sing, I thought, but just laid it to my general debility, such as no longer being able to run a mile in less than four minutes, or punt 90 yards into the wind consistently.

Then, one Sunday we got to church a little early, unaccountably, instead of a little late, and I began leafing through the hymn book. A couple of pages flipped by and suddenly there was "Let the Lower Lights Be Burning," a hymn my grandmother used to sing as she went about the house. A little further and there was "In the Garden," my father's favorite, and, one after another, all the old hymns thronging out of the pages, old friends holding out their hands in greeting. Excitedly, I counted 42 of them, enough, I told my wife, to gather in a book entitled, "Songs My Mother Taught Me That Nobody Sings Any More." Shush, she said.

I meant to talk with the pastor, who has answered all the other fool questions I've ever put to him, but didn't think about the subject until talking the other week by chance with a Methodist minister in Hanover county. Why don't we sing the OLD hymns anymore? I asked.

The way he explained it, the hymns of a generation ago were the NEW hymns, composed during the evangelical 1800's and under the impact of the Sunday School movement. Now the churches are returning to the truly old ones that carry a deeper message.

Many of the hymns of the 1800's, he noted, were directed at the individual, in a subjective way, where the earlier ones had tended to be to the glory of God. The trend to anthems and other older music is a part of the general effort at increasing our understanding.

I could see the sense of this, but the difficulty is that I can't disassociate the gospel numbers from those who enjoyed singing them so much. Just as the congregation reached the chorus, my grandmother would dip her hands slightly with the open hymnbook, as if summoning all the strength of body and soul to ring out her faith to the rafters, rejoicing. There was a sparkle in the old gray stone of the building, and as the congregation pealed forth, it seemed to me that the very stones were shining in song, calling to the passersby, a musical lifeline.

The hymns were so familiar that we knew them by their numbers. In Sunday school, when the song leader asked what shall we sing next, it sounded like an auction. No. 5 was "Love Lifted Me," I remember.

My grandmother was both a rock and a pillow to her large family. Her example, and that of the other good people, has become mixed in my memory with the hymns they sang seven days a week. I realize, thinking back, that some of the hymns were centered more on self than God, but generally, having sung them, you felt that you aimed to do better.

Many of the hymns, too, carried the sense of being joined in a great venture: "Bringing in the Sheaves," "There's a Land Beyond the River," "Onward Christian Soldiers," "When the Roll Is Called Up Yonder," "There's a Land That Is Fairer Than Day," "Rescue the Perishing," "Throw Out the Lifeline."

Of course, the musical programs of today's churches are miles ahead of those other times. I wish that my grandmother could hear the great choirs and the fine instrumental music. But, I wish, too, occasionally that the congregations could roll out again on one of the surging gospel hymns, EVERYBODY singing, a great, moving, buoyant ocean of faith.

---

## RIDDLES FOR BREAKFAST

Nothing like a calm breakfast to get in the mood for Monday, I thought.

The three boys were eating quietly, the oldest even reading a book at his elbow.

You mustn't put off your homework until the last thing Monday, I told him severely (thinking, desperately, about the column that had to be done by nine o'clock, and nothing in sight.)

He looked up from the book and asked: If a cork and a bottle cost $2.10, and the bottle cost $2.00 more than the cork, what does the cork cost?

Ten cents, I said promptly.    That's much too easy for the third grade.

Wrong, he said. The cork costs 5 cents, and the bottle costs $2.05.

I was never good at arithmetic, I told my wife, and now I've got to flunk it again, THREE TIMES.

If 10 birds were sitting on a telephone wire, and you shot one how many would remain? asked the boy.

It begins with an N, he said, helpfully.

NINE, I said, lunging.

None, he said, because they would all fly away.

DID YOU HEAR THAT? I asked my wife. Did you hear what they're teaching in school nowadays? Give me another, I told the boy.

What did Benjamin Franklin say when he discovered electricity in lightning?

I stared at the egg on my plate. It stared back. Unblinking.

I was pretty good in history, I said.

Stop stalling, said my wife. What's the answer?

Eureka, I said. I-have-found-it!

Wrong again, said the boy.

So what did he say? I asked.

Nothing. He was too shocked.

Will you have an egg? asked my wife.

I already had one, I said.

Will you have an egg? she asked again, looking at me steadily.

Look, I said, this family, all at once, is going question wild. I just told you, I ALREADY HAD AN EGG.

Will-you-have-an-egg? she persisted.

Look, Honey, I said, patiently, one egg is about my limit, but if you would care to inquire as to whether I wish more, then ask me, plainly, Will you have ANOTHER egg?

And may I suggest to you, she replied, that Emily Post says you should never ask anyone to have ANOTHER because that points out that the person has already had one.

I don't need Emily Post to tell me how to get eggs for breakfast, but between you and Emily Post, and this boy's teacher, I don't know whether I'm eating eggs or cocoanuts.

Every morning Farmer Brown had eggs for breakfast, said the boy, but he didn't own any chickens, and he never got eggs from chickens owned by anyone. Where did he get the eggs?

I don't know, I give up.

From his ducks, said the boy. They were duck eggs!

What did the ghost have for breakfast? he went on, quickly.

It beats me, I said. This whole discussion beats me.

Ghost toasties, said the boy.

LET ME SEE THAT BOOK, I shouted.

He handed it over. "Jokes and Riddles," it said. "For Boys and Girls."

Well, I said, anyway the school system is safe.

Will you have an egg? asked my wife.

---

# DAY'S CATCH

We spent the week end at Cole's Point on the Potomac River. From the talk passed around, on fishing, it might have been Texas.

The subject of fishing is new to me so I only half-believe any of it . . . such as the item mentioned by a fellow Richmonder, Roy O. Mann, that a fishing boat will sometimes tow a huge mower back and forth through seawood-choked water and then give it a day or two to clear away before dropping the nets. If that is not a tall tale—lawn-mowing the sea—it should be.

But I can vouch for one story that took place Friday afternoon.

Another Richmonder, George Taylor, came hurrying to where we were staying and called, Let's go see them All Saints.

Wait 'til I put on my shoes, I shouted. (If he wishes to go to church on Friday, I thought, then I will walk the second mile with any man and even a third with a friend.)

Don't bother about the shoes, he called. The fish won't mind.

By dint of keeping my mouth shut for 15 minutes I discovered we were not going to see them All Saints. We were going to see them haul seines.

It restored my faith in Taylor's grammar.

The way they All Saints—that is, HAUL SEINES, is anchor one end of the net to the shore and then a tug-size boat, with a little cabin amidships, chugs out about the length of six football fields, playing out the net as it goes, as if it were throwing a lasso around the area.

Three small open boats—only a little larger than those in Byrd Park lake—work around the fringes, seeing that the weights keep one edge of the net on the bottom and the quart-size corks keep the other edge afloat, to make a gradually closing wall around the fish.

On one of the boats—the donkey boat—a winch draws the net tighter around the enclosure, like boys playing "territory" with a jack-knife, until finally, the men slosh around in the water, pulling the net by hand, and then, using hand-nets on poles, scooping up gleaming fish as if they were shoveling coal.

The captain, Bill Hundley, was a slight, pleasant-faced man with blue eyes in bright contrast to the bronze-red of his face, cured by a lifetime of sun, salt, and Southwesterns. He may be 30 or 40 or 50, but in any case he has worked the sea since he was nine.

The catch was more fish than I had ever seen, but Hundley said it was a small one.

It was a losing game with us today, he said.

Not for us, said a big city fellow, moving forward with his wife to shake the captain's hand.

The seine boats, it turned out, had arrived just in time to pick up the couple's teen-age son who was being pulled out to sea by a treacherous crosscurrent off a sandbar extending into the Potomac.

It had happened before off that point, said Hundley, where the current, a swirling scoop, sweeps the sand from beneath a swimmer's feet and pulls him away so that while the swimmer thinks he is making time he is steadily losing ground.

Usually the seine boat works at night, and this Friday was only the second time this summer that Hundley had taken the boats out during the day, coming for the first time in a long time to the very point where the boy was being swept away.

Today, I think, was God-sent, said Hundley.

------

# THE HILL THAT GREW

With the first flake of snow, the three boys clamored to go sleighing on the hills by the river.

Crunching across the white plains, gently tilted, you get a sense of release in limitless space. The snow plays tricks with perspective. A near rise white-masked, becomes as remote as the Antarctic. A far flat, down by the river, is thrust into your face as if through an old-fashioned stereopticon.

Groups dotted the fields from all directions, ants moving over the white sheen of a damask cloth. In one band was an eager-faced boy, running up to those returning, shouting, Is it good? Is it good?

Shut up, stupid, his brother kept telling him, but the boy continued to dance around like an excited terrier, half-fearful that when he got to the hills the snow would somehow vanish and maybe the hills, too.

But there they were, in great penmanship loops, falling over each other whitely, leveling off briefly just before the canal. Four sleds already went in, piped a small boy.

Viewed from one hill, the white side of another was spread out all scarred with sled runners and pitted and pocked with footprints as if it carried some fantastic cuneiform message.

The Big Hill dropped down so fast on its steepest side that, standing at the top, watching climbers approach its base, you saw them vanish below you when they reached the middle part of the hill and then reappear after many seconds, panting, at the top. Fathers coming to the edge of the Big Hill for the first time, off the flat table-land, would look down and say with false heartiness, SAY-Y-Y-Y, this IS a hill ALL RIGHT.

I knew how they felt.

It's even worse than last year, I thought, when the sled rode ME down. You'd think a little erosion would set in around here, but this hill has GROWN.

One more year, and it'll be a confounded mountain.

It almost is NOW.

Boys, boys, I said, let's go home and make some fudge.

But no, they were looking down, jaws set, so I sat on the sled, my arms around the 7-year-old, my feet on the guide bar, my hands on the rope, my heart in my mouth.

Now, I said to the 9-year-old, Give us a little nudge . . . A NUDGE I SAID, NOT A PUSH! CUT-OUT-THAT-PUSH-ING!

Off we went.

Talk about astronauts!

By George, I thought, this is going to confuse things in Washington AND Mosocow when I hit the moon with a sled.

Make Wernher von Braun look like a fool with his rockets. Faster and faster.

Put down your feet, you fool. Brake this thing.

I did, and two huge spumes of snow rose all around us. The sled sped along in white clouds of chilly glory. An astonished teen-ager, standing on the side, yelled something as we shot by.

LOOK AT OLD VAPOR TRAILS! he shouted.

Then we were at the bottom, overturned, laughing, in a surf of snow.

I gave up, generously, all the rest of my turns.

Later, at home, my wife asked, How was it?

It was like a band playing in front of us all the way down, all that snow flying, said the 7-year-old.

What's he talking about? she asked.

It beats me, I said. You know how kids are.

I had to turn my head, said the boy.

What ever does he mean? she asked.

Think nothing of it, I said.

----

# FINIS, ALMOST

Soon, in a magic moment, Conductor Edgar Schenkman will raise his arms in front of the Richmond Symphony and a deep contest of wits will begin between him and me. Or at least I see it that way.

The idea is to catch Friddell clapping in the wrong place. I have carried on the same not-so-silent duel with Ormandy and scores of others.

The conductor will bring down his hands in a crashing, head-shaking crescendo—like Samson pulling down the pillars—and let them hang limp at his sides, head bowed.

It is over.

The whole orchestra is sitting in stunned silence.

It is ended.

Finis, as they say in Bon Air.

Any fool could see it.

So I begin clapping and IMMEDIATELY the conductor raises his hands and has the orchestra galloping off on another rondu, or whatever it is that orchestras gallop off on. (Certainly not two prepositions.)

But they do not gallop away before everybody has heard three or four lonely thunder-claps from that dunce perched up in the rafters of the last row. There's no lonelier sound in the world than to find yourself clapping BY YOURSELF in the midst of 5,000 people, all looking at you in ill-disguised disgust. I've even had people move away, as if a dam had burst and water was rising around their ankles.

Run for the hills everybody. That mad fool is clapping in the wrong place.

Under any conditions I'm the loudest applauder. None of this pitty-pat for me. If the boys in the pit, sawing away at violins, tooting on horns, have earned an accolade, then let 'em hear it.

Let everybody passing outside on the street hear it, too, through the brick walls, and make them wish they were inside, the soreheads.

Send the sound waves all the way to Short Pump. Drown out the trucks in Ginter Park. Put Sandston on the alert, and bring South Richmond running to the banks of the river.

That's the way to applaud.

Loud.

Not loudly. LOUD.

Cup your hands just slightly and pound the palms into each other, crossways, thumbs overlapping.

Once my wife sat downstairs (through some mix-up on her part too illogical to go into here), and she reported that amid the heaviest applause, when EVERYBODY was clapping, she could still hear me above all the others. You clown, she said.

I met Schenkman on the street the other day. Does it bother you when people clap in the wrong place? I asked.

He smiled. I'm delighted, he said. It means that someone in the audience is hearing the piece for the first time. It is my privilege to introduce him to it.

Schenkman is tops.

I shall go hear him tonight.

And clap TWICE AS LOUD.

In the wrong place.

# TO BE IN, COOK OUT

The cookout finally got me.

All you do, everybody said, is light the charcoal, throw on a steak, and it's all over. It very nearly was.

First, the matches wouldn't strike. They were the new-fangled, pasteboard kind that will strike only on their special box, and the children had emptied them in my shoe and gone off with the box they knew not where.

I spent 45 minutes trying to strike matches and at last, standing in the middle of the back yard, I yelled: Honey, the forces of communism have taken over the entire match industry, and are trying to drive us into frustration by producing matches that won't strike.

She went next door and borrowed a match box. It's a point of honor with me not to seek help from the neighbors in these bouts with the machine age, so she goes.

Another habit of mine is not to read directions. I used most of the matches before learning you must first douse the charcoal with lighter fluid. I learned that only because the neighbor to my right threw a can of fluid over the fence in my direction, being careful not to speak.

Still disdaining tedious instructions (the only instructions I try to read on a can are those printed in Spanish), I sprayed on lighter fluid, struck a match, and sure enough, up flared a blaze—and died down. The neighbor to my left stuck his head out the back door and called, "Let it soak," and then ducked back inside.

Indeed, left unlit for a spell, the charcoal absorbed the fluid and then, when lit, burned steadily. I jacked up the grill away from the sleepy coals, threw on the steak, and strolled humming inside where my wife was telling out-of-town guests at some filling station or other how to find us.

I'm going to the corner for rolls, I said, keep an eye on the old-cookout.

I left, with her on the phone, the steak on the grill, thinking surely all was right with the world. It just shows how quick the scene can change.

Returning, I found my wife dancing around the grill, waving a spatula at flames that were leaping three feet into the air. She looked like Salome in the fire dance.

Honey, I called, that is no way to conduct yourself. Stop putting on dramatics with the cookout. Give me the spatula.

No, I said, on second thought, go get a six-foot shovel, for it will take that to reach through this fiery funace and turn the steak. Better still, I called, as she was searching under the house for the shovel that was in the ditch out front, better still, bring the garden hose, and bring it fast because it appears to me that this tree is going to go next.

(The leaves were beginning to wither in the crown of the 30-foot oak under which I had place the cookout.)

Quick, I called, Quick, honey, turn the hose on the cookout.

The stream of water hit the flames. From the dense clouds of steam rolling around, you'd have thought the Old 97 had wrecked right in our back yard. There was a honking out front, and my wife cried, Gracious, the guests, and went running to meet them.

I pried what was left of the steak from the grill.

Our friends were not exactly ecstatic, but they were curious, politely.

But what IS it? they kept asking. It has such a distinctive FLAVOR, they kept saying, working their mouths.

How ever did you catch this taste of a charred, water-soaked building? they asked, tears starting in their eyes.

Well, I conceded, it wasn't easy but if you want just a hint, read Charles Lamb's "Dissertation on Rost Pig."

---

# THE COOL MEN

There's a new American hero coming out of the space age, and he doesn't look anything like Troy or Tab or Rock or Fabian or any of those glamor boys on television. He looks like the ordinary house-holder down the street going to work. He looks like Every Man.

Those seven astronauts—at first glance, anyway—are about the most down-to-earth guys you ever saw. As each takes his place in the capsule, it's interesting to watch the details of his personality grow in our national consciousness—Shepard, cocky, gamin in public and then, at the console controls, his bulbous features becoming almost truculent; Grissom, looking about as dramatic as a slightly moody Garry Moore.

The new hero looks as every day as your neighbor until you begin to read about him and find that his mind ranges at the genius level, he can run 100 yards in 10 seconds, or sit for three hours strapped on a contour couch, waiting for the blast-off, conversing by telephone with his wife and boys, telling them calmly at one point that if they don't stop talking he'll never go to sleep.

That's another thing. They're all married men, with hostages to fortune. On television, the Western hero rides off into the sunset, or the private eye watches a beautiful girl switch out of the bar and his life, but when they fish Grissom out of the sea, he goes home to Betty and the boys.

Still further, they manage—the seven of them—to pull off the old American miracle of remaining intensely individual, but working smoothly—almost affectionately—as a team. They're cool as a group of draughtsman working out a problem on the drawing board. They have the esprit of a patrol behind enemy lines thinking more of each other than of the place of any one of them in history.

That was a master-stroke, picking men of such brains and brawn that they could work with each other at every step in the project, with the public peering over their shoulders on TV at the climatic moments. All anybody has seen Gagarin do is kiss Gina Lollabrigida.

It's more understandable now, that press officer for our astronauts, who snapped that everybody was asleep when a reporter called at 3 a.m. on the morning Gagarin was orbited. Those seven have never doubted our ability to win the race the Soviets selected and started in secret.

We'll be licked in other laps through space, but there's a feeling the country can take temporary reverses without undue flap.

The machines are marvelous, but the seven men who ride them sum up in themselves the honest and best qualities Americans like to think are in the national character. Through history there's been talk of super men. These are seven super normal men, taking their flights through space with grit, competence and humor.

# A CAROM ON THE BRINK

Out at our house right now it's caroms. A friend gave the the boys the game last Christmas and all during the holiday we thumped the red and green rings across the big board into the little green mesh pockets at the corners. Then the carom board sort of drifted into the attic.

That's a system my wife uses. When she senses that a game has reached the point where it's about to be broken over somebody's head, she spirits it away to the attic. Six months later, stumbling around in the frozen tundra up there in search of a curtain rod, one of the boys comes across the carom board and shouts, HEY, LOOK WHAT I FOUND! as if he is Cortez discovering the misplaced Pacific.

Suddenly the game is new all over. There's a fresh run on it. We all go carom mad again. I do not know how my wife figured out this system. Maybe it is intuitive, like a bird building a nest, to hide things in the attic. But it works.

I suggested last year, just after Christmas, that we take ALL the toys up there, remove the ladder, and not bring them down until next Christmas.. Somehow what I was planning got out and a delegation of merchants from Exciting Downtown Richmond and the Outer Banks of Suburbia paid me an official visit in striped pants. Don't do this to the nation, they pleaded. The attic method, if carried to extremes, would wreck the free enterprise system AND Santa Claus. Don't put Santa in the attic, they begged.

I graciously agreed to let my wife continue to handle the attic traffic, on the sheer migratory instinct, and the other day one of the boys found the carom board.

The two older ones "stood" me and the five-year-old. Each has a distinctive style of shooting. The oldest snaps the shooter fiercely, directly, at top speed—zip, wham, bang. The middle boy lounges up to the board sideways, a Mississippi gambler, and flips his index finger at the shooter with an almost insolent soft touch. The youngest, my partner, has no discernible system. Competing with his older brothers, he is as taut, as trembling as an over-drawn bow, and when he shoots, his shooter is likely to fly across the room and land in the bookcase.

As he bent to aim, his older brothers would cover their heads and cower in mock terror. On the verge of tears of exasperation, he would miss and send his shooter spinning into the pocket while the other two danced in glee at the extra carom we had to put on the board as a penalty. It went that way most of the afternoon—my knocking them in the pocket, the five-year-old putting them back on the board—until finally, just before supper, the game had worked down to where we had only one carom left to sink and our opponents, the dancing savages, had two remaining on the board. Our last carom was perched right on the brink of the pocket, impossible it seemed for the shooter to tap in without following it for a penalty. It was the five-year-old's turn to shoot.

AT THAT MOMENT their mother began calling them to supper while, she said, the waffles are hot, as if anybody gave a hang about a hot waffle with the five-year-old bending to shoot while his brothers screeched and wig-wagged their hands over the board.

I'LL POKE THE FIRST ONE THAT TOUCHES THAT BOARD, I shouted. DON'T LET THEM EXCITE YOU, I yelled at my partner. BE CALM, BE CALM, IT'S NOTHING BUT A GAME. THIS IS THE SHOT THAT COUNTS, BUT DON'T WORRY, DON'T GET EXCITED.. JUST TAKE YOUR TIME AND —

About then, bending in white concentrated fury over the board, he shot. His marker slithered across the board, just touched the carom poised on the lip of the cup, tapped it in, and the shooter skidded to a stop precisely on the edge, safe. The stunned silence that followed was the sweetest sound of the week end.

---

# SHOLOM, THAT MEANS PEACE

There was an empty booth about the size of a piano crate out on the edge of the sidewalk and a middle-age man looking at it carefully, from a distance. Shoppers streamed along between the two, unaware a meeting of significance was going on between the man and the booth.

The man walked closer to the open, empty booth, and studied the sign that said today the Salvation Army Kettle Booth was manned by B'nai B'rith, Rimmon Dominion Lodge.

In a moment, along with three red buckets hanging by silver chains, the sign, and a bell the booth held Ernest Gunzburg.

A Salvation Army officer, strapped Santa-tight in his uniform, instructed Gunzburg just as he had done dozens of nervous businessmen from other service organizations. Some have said they never felt as helpless as when they first took that mike and started to speak to hundreds of people, hurrying, it seemed, to catch a train somewhere. It hits you just where you start to breathe, one said.

Gunzburg clutched the mike like a man who feels he maybe has hooked a whale by mistake.

"Will you help us . . . to help others . . . for Christmas?" he asked the crowd surging below his booth.

Nobody looked up.

"Let this be a happiness holiday," he pleaded.

There was a plunk in the bucket.

"God bless you," he said.

Gunzburg stuck to his quiet, earnest S.O.S.

"Let's help these poor people," he would say, and, coming out over Broad Street, sounding faintly through the door of the busy department store, it sounded almost as if he had them lined up out there with him along the sidewalk in rags.

"It will be good, giving," he called to the crowd, and a defiant-faced teen-ager, "Whitey," broke away from a half-dozen others contorted with merriment, and dropped a dime in the bucket.

"God bless you, my boy. You'll have a Merry Christmas," said Gunzburg. In seconds, the others followed.

From time to time he saw an acquaintance in the throng. One paused, listened critically, and then said something.

"He corrected my English," Gunzburg said cheerfully. "You see I'm not a native Richmonder. I'm from Germany."

The friend thought Gunzburg's way of saying "kettle" could be improved.

A passing mistletoe merchant tossed a sprig on the counter, and Gunzburg twined it in the chain of the center kettle.

"Let this be a merry Christmas to all," he urged.

Two beggars approached, one playing a banjo, the other holding a tin cup.

"Competition," commented Gunzburg in an aside, with a wide, shy smile. He waited politely until they had passed.

"Let's everybody have a holiday with happiness," he called.

His plea touched a stout man, charging down the sidewalk, a big, big operator out to do his shopping in one swoop. He came back, chewing a ciger thoughtfully, pushed a bill through the grill. When he left, it was at an amble.

By now Gunzburg was ringing the bell vigorously, and the booth was a boat bobbing in a sea of Christmas mirth.

"Come over here and fill these kettles with happiness," he called.

A large man, with remote eyes in a mahogany hard face, dropped an offering, and when Gunzburg thanked him, a smile split his face like a creek flashing through a dry land.

Gunzburg couldn't see some of the appreciative smiles that followed his benedictions, but one woman, white-haired, looked up at him and said, quite clearly, "Thank you for the privilege of giving."

Children's face floated below the kettle, smiling, shining, brighter than Christmas stamps. One, going away, asked her mother if he were Santa Claus.

"What a wonderful feeling, to place your gifts in the kettle," he called.

A leather-jacketed sport came to the kettle with an embarrassed swagger. A young woman, her hair skinned back in a tight bun, fumbling with bundles, dropped coins, cigaret ashes, and all her composure in the kettle, and fled, laughing, her sophistication lost. Sober, dignified businessmen bumped through the jostling crowd, absent-minded but compelled by his bell and plea. A woman, in furs, hurrying by, missed his plea, but the child at her side looked back with a face alive with interest.

A Negro woman, large and awkward, in a frayed black coat, took a half dollar from a shiny, green plastic purse. Gunzburg said softly some of those giving ought to be getting.

His relief failed to appear, but Gunzburg stayed.

"It's no use doing it," he told the Salvation Army man, "unless you do it right. You don't do it half-hearted."

Toward the close of the long afternoon, he spied a friend, waiting for the traffic light down the street.

"A happy holiday to you, Martha," he called.

She looked up, her face bewildered at the greeting that came winging above the Broad st. traffic. Then, seeing him smiling in the booth, she hurried back, her hand outstretched.

"Merry Christmas . . . Sholom," she said.

"Sholom," replied Gunzburg. "That means peace, he explained to a bystander.

To the 5 o'clock crowd, surging by the little booth Gunzburg cried, "A happy holiday to all of you!"

---

# THE DAM IN CENTERFIELD

Here the New Year is only a week old, and yesterday I learned how to throw a football. The 9-year-old taught me.

Get out and play with your children, the books say, if it breaks your neck.

After his twenty-first request (when I was really sure the boy meant it) I put down the paper and joined him in the front yard.

All these years I've been grabbing the football around the middle and flailing away in a wobbly end-around-end pass.

You're doing it wrong, he called.

Don't tell me how to throw a football, I yelled. All that kept me out of the Rose Bowl was a trick knee.

You're supposed to hold it back nearer the end, he called. Let the weight in the nose guide it.

After a couple more dignified failures my own way, I tried his style, and, sure enough, it worked.

It was his grandfather who taught him how to throw it Christmas, the sneak. You'd think he'd show ME, but no, they like to pass those secrets on to alternate generations.

The subject of athletics is beginning to get a little sticky around my house anyway.

When I was shaving this morning, the five-year-old marched in and said, Guybo, when did you play baseball?

Oh, a long time ago.

But WHEN?

I dread for him to find out when.

When was when the boys in my neighborhood played the Hollow Gang and had to have nine players. They stuck me in centerfield, way out where they figured I'd do the least damage, and the rightfielder played in toward the middle.

There was lots to do out there. You could sit on a rock and fish for tiger worms with a wild onion stalk. Sometimes I'd sit four innings at a stretch in the lazy sun, not even bothering to go into bat or even get up untill somebody slammed the ball over my head. It was a depressing sight, that ball bouncing away toward the pasture creek like a hopped-up rabbit, and hard to find, like an old moss-stained boulder.

I'd poke around down in the creek, out of sight, and presently notice how a big rock placed at just the right angle would change the course of the channel and then add a little sand and blue clay from the bank and you got the start of a dam and then put this rock over here, by George, and—

About that time there'd be a shout from the bank above, and I'd see the heads of the other two fielders dark against a white-spun cloud.

Come on down, I'd yell, and give me a hand with this confounded creek.

They'd slide down the bank and the three of us would work like fury hauling sand, moss, and rock until up in the pasture somebody would send the shortstop to find what was delaying us. Then the first baseman would come to check on HIM and then the pitcher because it was HIS baseball, and pretty soon there'd be 18 of us down there in the cool water building that old dam.

I was a great centerfielder.

# THE KITE THAT HAD IT

Some kind-hearted person gave us a kite, the kind that gets hung in trees.

When are we going to put it up? shouted the three boys.

Right now, I said. We are going to put it up in the hall closet and fly it in April, that great kite-flying month.

For shame, said my wife.

I never saw such a kite.

Beautifully colored, red white and blue.

Flimsy as tissue paper.

They don't makes kites like they used to, I said.

No, they don't, she agreed. I can remember MY father getting down on the kitchen floor with a bowl of flour paste and making a kite out of the Sunday newspaper.

I'll bet it's still there, I said, stuck to the kitchen floor.

You'd think it wouldn't take 45 minutes to cross and bend two sticks, but it did.

Now, boys, boys, I said, take the kite out front while I put on a sweater and DON'T LET THE DOG GET IT.

I opened the front door, and there, spread below, the dog— kite in mouth—was running around the yard like a brown-and-white comet chased by three laughing luniks.

He's small—part-beagle, part-basset—ideal, said his former owner, for chasing rabbits under bushes, or, as I saw, for running with a kite between the legs of small boys.

It's not that he's so fast. Like those compact cars, he has a small wheel base and can stop, start, turn on a dime, and run forever with a kite in his mouth.

I froze them with a shout and stalked down the steps, looking the dog straight in the eye, just like Carl Akeley says. At the bottom, I crouched and came across the yard on all fours, lifting one hand or foot at a time, slowly, surely, nearer and nearer while Thurber—that's the darned dog's name—his nose between his paws, watched me in cross-eyed craftiness.

MY eyes began to water. By George, I thought, Akeley never

came up against anything like THIS. But don't waver. Stare the beast down.

Three feet away I paused, braced for a spring, set to let out a lion-like roar and petrify him— when he dropped the kite, stepped forward and kissed me on the chops.

The kite was a sight. A sieve.

Go inside, I told the youngest, and tell your mother to send some of that great paste her kite-making father used and some rags for a tail.

She sent out a box of band-aids and a long gauzy pink ruffle off some gown. The Florence Nightingale of the kite world.

Now listen, I told the boys. This kite has already given as much excitement as any kite could. It cannot possibly take off and, even if it does, we are boxed in by trees and the house. Now you know the score. Let her go and don't expect anything.

But I had reckoned without one thing.

That kite had DESIRE.

Along with a lot of band-aids and a pink tail.

In a dogged way, it began to struggle up.

BY GEORGE, I shouted, SHE WANTS TO FLY. GIVE HER STRING.

I criss-crossed the yard, about the size of a large pool table, yanking on the string, leaping every three feet over a boy or a dog, and my wife stood at the front door calling, WATCH THE BANK! WATCH THE BANK!, and I yelled, FEED HER STRING! FEED HER STRING! FOR HEAVEN'S SAKE, FEED HER STRING! and the oldest shouted, WE CAN'T! WE CAN'T THE DOG HAS IT!, and the kite was pulling mightily, trying to climb. I tripped, and everybody was chasing the dog with the ball of cord in his mouth, and THE DOG WAS FLYING THE KITE! Through it all the kite climbed, a beautiful sight, straight over the house, so steadily that when we were all untracked, we sent up message. I even considered trying to send up the dog.

Look, boys, I said, this kite has earned its freedom. Let's turn her loose.

We did, and it went dropping down, wig-wagging toward the mist along the river. I turned to go inside, a little sadly, when

suddenly they began to shout. THE KITE! LOOK AT THE
KITE!

It was climbing, magically, on its own, pulling against the string
caught on some distant tree-top. It stood there, an eyelash against
the evening sky, until dark.

I never saw such a kite.

Determined to fly.

---

# THE SUNDAY SUIT

Face it, said my wife at breakfast this morning.

Face what? I asked, alarmed, wondering if she meant the day
ahead, life, or an affectionate child about to lay a jelly-smeared
hand on my collar.

You must buy a Sunday suit, she said.

Anybody who went through the Depression—that was the time
when suits were a dime a dozen and nobody had a dime—has what
he regards as a Sunday suit. This is the suit reserved for special
occasions. It is also the suit which, when you want it, is in the
cleaners.

You can almost count the Sunday suits, four or five in your
mind, life's geological strata in herringbone, tweed, and flannel.

The green one—from an end of the season basement sale—in
which you took out your first date and marched across the stage
for your high school diploma.

The gray flannel you bought with mustering out pay to apply
for a job.

The brown one, worn at the knees, in which you proposed.

The dark gray pinstripe your wife picked out for you after
the first raise.

It's a suit that has to be treated with tenderest care.

Look out, you yell to a child, You're dribbling jelly beans all
over my Sunday-suit.

Once, in a conference, I came out looking even worse than
usual because while everyone else was in deep discussion about the
topic at hand, I was trying to sit lightly on the edge of my chair

so as not to uncrease my Sunday suit.  The talk was droning along
when an energetic young executive said suddenly, "Let's bounce the
ball to Friddell."

I flinched.

He was only asking for my ideas, but for a wild moment I
thought he had smuggled a dirty old basketball into the conference
and was going to throw it on my Sunday suit.

My mind was running along these lines this morning when my
wife made her suggestion at the breakfase table.

I SAID, she said, a little impatient at my pensive air, I SAID
you need to get a new Sunday suit.

Why?  I wanted to know.

Well, you're going to follow Khrushchev for the next two weeks.
That's an occasion that should call for your best suit.

What!  I exclaimed in horror.  Listen, there are going to be
1,000 reporters trying to see Khrushchev, and I'm not going to take
my Sunday suit into that crush.

Go dig out my army fatigues, I said.

Let Khrushchev wear HIS Sunday suit.

---

# KHRUSHCHEV: LAST ACT

WASHINGTON, Sept. 28—The two men climbed the steps to
Blair House while the crowds behind ropes across the street strained
to see their faces.

At the door, President Eisenhower gestured toward the photo-
graphers calling below.  The pair faced the cameras.  The crowd
saw Premier Khrushchev smile, then saw Eisenhower give his
wide-mouthed grin, a news flash in itself.

The two shook hands and held the clasp as they talked.  Ike put
his hand on his heart.  Khrushchev plunged his hands stiffly at his
sides and moved them there in emphasis as if his words were wrung
from his depths.

Again they shook hands.  Ike turned to go, pausing at the bottom of the steps to call something about his bringing the whole
family.  He gave Khrushchev a little one-fingered salute.  The

Premier raised his arm in that coy, parasol way and waggled his hand. Both men were still smiling. That's how they said goodby in the September sun in front of Blair House.

From there Khrushchev set out for the National Press Club. About that time, testing acoustics in the auditorium, the club president was asking someone to call out a question.

"What day is it?" yelled a weary reporter.

"What YEAR is it?" called another.

Then Khrushchev was on stage, all business, in a deep blue suit, accented by gold medals, gold-rimmed glasses, and a gold tooth. A tiny, self-assured smile played on his thick lips. He looked from side to side while the cameras flashed.

"Ho-kay! Ho-kay!" he said. The cameras stopped and the questions began. There was nothing in them to bring out the snake look, the sudden thrusting forward of his head at the crowd, the tightening of his lips (as wide on a line as the expanse of his small, narrow-set eyes) that made him appear sometimes an angry boa constrictor. Soviet Deputy Foreign Minister V. V. Kuznetsov screened the questions.

Early in his tour Khrushchev established the ground rules, at the cost of refusing to play, that exchanges had to proceed from the moment at hand, from NOW. If there were to be a happy ending, unpleasant things in the Russian past were a closed chapter.

He stood before them, a tanned tenpin, impossible to knock down. His bald head and tanned face rose on a thick neck from his low-cut collar like a fist. The nose was sharply aggressive, the mouth that of a stump politician, the upper lip tight drawn, the lower lip thick and broad to the point that it almost looked carved in repose, the jaw underslung for marathon conversations.

At times he exuded cannibalistic good humor, even more alarming than his barking wrath, as when a reporter asked him to explain the numbers of young people attending church in Russia.

Mere curiosity, much as your youths would turn out to see me, said Khrushchev, over the space of five minutes, leaning forward, his beady eyes darting, his wet smile loose- lipped, as if he would like to reach out and wrap the questioner in an all-embracing togetherness.

His next stop was a television station, where he said that the Soviet Union was going to build 50 San Franciscos in seven years.

Then Khrushchev headed for the Andrews Air Force Base. More than a dozen searchlights put a blue pallor in the sky from a distance and cast a sunset glow on the spot where Khrushchev was to give his ego a last, lingering public bathing.

The same Pfc. was sweeping the 150-foot red carpet, only this time he had to go only halfway to where it vanished into the gloom of the landing field.

Waiting were Vice-President Nixon and Dresden-cool Pat, craggy-faced Herter, a worn looking Lodge, and Soviets headed by Menshikov, faintly smiling.

Khrushchev, staight-backed, melon-bellied, met each with a handshake and precise tiny bow, like a billiken. Then they proceeded to the podium, about the size of a diving platform. Nixon praised the moonshot, marveled at Khrushchev's vitality. Khrushchev held up his hand and looked into the kleig lights.

When his time came, he half-turned as if he didn't know where to stand, put on his glasses as if they were radioactive, and finally took out his speech and looked at it as if it were a dead fish somebody had stuck in his pocket. Then, having extracted all he could from the moment, he read the speech. He said he hoped that "ho-kay" would be heard more and more often in business between the two nations.

Someone put a huge bouquet of red roses in his bear-like arms, and he was off waddling down the reception line. No, he wasn't. He was all fouled up in the frazzled start of the line, greeting people, chatting as if he were just arriving.

Some diplomat got him on track again, and he moved along on his stubby legs, beaming, shaking hands, and vanished into the darkness, holding an enormous, towering bouquet of roses over his bald head.

Mir y Dhrzba!

## HOW TO BE SUAVE AND SOP

A reader writes to report that he is going to a formal dinner in a couple of weeks and asks me if he should sop any gravy or juices left in his plate.

"I am writing you," he says, "because you look just fool enough to have tried it."

Well, thank you for your confidence.

About this time of year the hostess will be serving, probably, corn cut fresh off the cob and allowed to simmer in a big iron skillet on top of the stove; crisp, salty streaker-lean-streaker-fat bacon; cucumbers and onions sliced thin in iced vinegar: great red slabs of beefsteak tomatoes with a little left-over red-eye ham gravy poured over them; smoking hot cornbread, with lots of country butter, and iced tea sporting a sprig of mint.

Near the end, the juices of all those fresh vegetables will begin to blend and swim in the plate in a spirit of togetherness, and it would make a man cry to leave them there, the meal's essence.

I don't know how this sham started anyway, that it was impolite to sop. True epicureans—going back to Henry VIII and Louis XIV—have always sopped. It's a tribute to the kitchen.

But, PLEASE, dear reader, try to be a little subtle in how you go about it. In an absentminded way, in the heat of a discussion on politics or crabgrass, sort of lay the cornpone in the bottom of the plate, where the juices are, and presently look down, and say, By George! I haven't finished my cornpone!

Then pick up your fork and start to spear the cornpone but FUMBLE, so that the fork falls to the floor. As your hostess starts to get up or rings for another fork, you say, No bother, I'll just eat it as is.

Some people will tell you that it unnerves them to sop in strange company, but this is nonsense. Etiquette is nothing but doing what comes most naturally, in the easiest, lest conspicuous way, and after you drop the fork, everyone is relieved when you simply pick up the cornpone and eat. I've dropped a fork as much as six times in a single meal to keep people around me at ease.

# SHE LOVES ME, SHE . . .

I went back to high school the other day, and they were still signing annuals, just as when I left 20 years ago.

My teachers were as young, as shining-eyed as ever with ambition for others. (One student got a half year's credit when he entered M. I. T. for high school work in calculus with analytical geometry.)

We can thank sputnik for that," said my geomety teacher. "Almost overnight sputnik brought us that for which we had been fighting for 20 years—books and unlimited scope for advancing the gifted student."

Used to be, she said, all the stress was devoted to helping the poor student, but no longer.

I got out just in time.

But the annuals hadn't changed . . .

The same deathless messages—"Don't do anything I wouldn't do (The sky's the limit.)" . . . "Will you ever forget that 'easy' algebra course?" . . . "Think of me in sixth period study hall!" . . . and whole pages of vows to eternity between the girls.

Just as it was 20 years ago, and 20 years before that, except for an occasional bit of slang: "We've really had a blast this year."

It stirred in my memory an event I thought I'd never forget. . . .

She was, I thought, the prettiest girl in the high school that had the prettiest girls in the world.

Day after day in the cafeteria at lunch time I tried to dazzle her with words and antics, most of which I'd laboriously worked out the night before. (I should heve devoted more time to dazzling my algebra teacher who very nearly flunked me in June.)

A smile from her and I was like an old collie of mine who at the sight of me would go into every trick he knew—lie down, roll over, shake hands, "speak," and play dead.

The day the annuals came out I said this is the test. If I've made any impression, if she has the slightest regard for me, she will say so in signing the annual.

I stood by as she signed, noting with delight she was writing a good deal more than "Best of Luck." She handed me the closed book with the smile that shed a stained glass radiance. I stammered my thanks and walked dazedly away.

Around the corner, in the hurrying hubbub of the hall, I hastily opened the book to her picture and read what she had written.

There they were, in her wispy hand, the words that (so I thought) I would never forget:

"You nutty thing. I don't believe I have ever met a boy half as nutty as you, and I don't think I ever will. You were always good for a laugh."

It was plain. She cared.

---

# THIS HERE, THAT THERE

When the army issued carbines to my outfit, Sergeant Maypop almost exploded.

Just when we were winning the war, he said, meaning the country was winning it, not the outfit.

Only after returning to civilian life did I understand how mnch Sergeant Maypop had meant to us. Indeed, it has been as he predicted: Youse guys are going to miss me.

We were all 4-F's, except the sergeant, and in moments of stress he would bellow: I don't know why the army brought yers together, but I'm going to get yers home safely, if I have to kill every one of yers to do it and don't try to stop me.

When the army announced that it was going to place guns in our hands, Sergeant Maypop said he was going to take them right out again and lock them up.

He did let an ordnance officer come before us in the mess hall and name the parts of the carbine all the way down to the "sear", a tiny catch, scarcely larger than an eyelash, in the trigger assembly.

The officer was at the far end of the dim mess hall, talking suddenly about the sear, holding up nothing as far as I could see, and every time he said "the sear," I thought he was saying "this here."

Boy, I thought, that's just like the army. Send a supposed expert to tell us about the carbine and for all the expert knows he can only say 'this here' and 'that there'.  What a way to run a war!

When the ordnance officer finished, Sergeant Maypop, standing hands clasped behind his back like Napoleon at Elba, said he would ask a few questions in review.

Friddell, the sergeant yelled.  What is the sear?

He caught me flat-footed.  I thought Sergeant Maypop, in a commendable effort to lighten what had been a dull demonstration, was hiding something behind his back, as children do, and wanted me to guess what it was.  The old brain, clicking all the time, told me he was probably holding a vegetable from the kitchen.  If he wants to play games, I thought then Sherlock Friddell is ready.

FRIDDELL! roared the sergeant again.  I see yers hiding back there in the darkness.  What is the sear?

AN IRISH POTATO!  I roared back, with conviction.

There was silence, then a crash of applause from my comrades . . . Guessed right, by George, the first time, I thought, but no, the sergeant was bellowing to me above the tumult.

Friddell, youse mad fool, before it's too late: WHAT IS THE SEAR?

A SWEET potato, I called.

I'll give yers one last chance before the court martial, roared Sergeant Maypop.  NOW . . . WHAT . . . IS . . . THE-SEAR?

A rutabaga! I yelled.

That was wrong, too.  Later, after the ordnance officer departed, looking pale, Sergeant Maypop called me to headquarters tent.  He was surprisingly benign.

Well, he said, I will hand it to yers.  You convinced one member of the brass that this outfit wasn't ready for firearms.

You mean they're going to take away our guns?  I asked.

We can keep the guns, he said, but they're NOT going to give us any ammunition.

Sergeant Maypop, I asked, what WERE you holding behind your back?

# I'M WATCHING YOU, DISNEY

Used to be (before television) psychologists said the mental age of the movie-goer was 14.

You can cut that by half for me.

The five of us went to the movies the other day. Hardest hit were the 7-year-old and me. Or is it I?

Even as we entered there was a panicky bit when we got separated in the darkness.

For Pete's sake, I ordered a passing usher, help me find my wife.

Is she lost? he asked.

No, but I am.

He disappeared, and in a moment boomed over the loudspeaker: WILL THE YOUNG LADY WHO MISPLACED HER HUSBAND PLEASE CLAIM HIM AT THE POPCORN CONCESSION?

More embarrassment as we sidled to our seats.

HERE? I called to her. No, she said, keep moving. NOW? I called. Don't sit in the lady's lap, she said. Keep going.

At one point, positive we were on target, I reached down to feel for the face of one of my young ones.

A rough, bearded face . . . (Strange, I thought, how quickly children grow and get away from you) . . . and thick, horn-rimmed glasses. (That shouldn't be, should it?) . . . Gin, I called in the darkness, correct me if I'm wrong, but does one of our boys wear horn-rims? . . . A big ear, and just about then a voice growled, Mac, I swear if you put your finger in my mouth I'LL BITE IT OFF.

The movie was about a little boy who ran away to the circus and made friends with a monkey because his uncle yelled at him.

Praise be, Disney made him an uncle, I thought.

A hunter shot the monkey out of a tree, by mistake.

By George, I thought, how cold-hearted can Hollywood get? Leave this sort of thing to those prize-winning Italian films. You'd think Disney would understand that children, not hunters, were coming to see this movie.

The little boy on the screen sobbed over the still monkey.

I looked to check how my boys were taking this. First I had to wipe my eyes.

The 9-year-old was glaring at the screen. The 4-year-old had gone to sleep. The 7-year-old was batting his eyes furiously.

Don't cry, I said, trying not to sob too loudly. Everything will be all right, I choked.

Is the monkey dead?

DON'T WORRY ABOUT IT, I said. The monkey had a full, happy life. Just one big circus.

Is he dead?

Of course not, I said. This is only a movie.

But is he dead in the movie.

LISTEN, I said, he's playing possum. HE-IS-NOT-DEAD. (But quick as I can hitch-hike to Hollywood, Disney's going to be.)

They left the monkey in the woods.

I still think he's dead, said the 7-year-old.

But—SURPRISE—when Toby Tyler opened the tent flap, THERE WAS THE MONKEY, bandaged but alive. A little later when Toby was riding bareback, as I used to do in my dreams, the monkey sneaked out and dropped from a tentpole onto his shoulders. Everybody laughed and clapped, even the ornery uncle.

I looked down. Both the 7-year-old and I were clapping.

As we rode home, the boy said. That was a good movie, wasn't it?

Excellent, I said.

It was very good about the monkey, he said.

It was, I said.

Weren't you glad? he asked.

I'll say, I said.

It's a long way to Hollywood, hitch-hiking.

---

# THE FREE (SHOELESS) PRESS

The 7-year-old broke his shoe lace dressing for the first day of school.

It caused more outcry then the fall of a Summit because he is unusually careful in his dress, compensating for his father, I guess.

There was no time to go to the store, and, with Einstein inspiration, I pulled out my shoe laces and gave them to him. From the look on his face, you'd have thought I'd put the Summit together again.

I'll buy a pair on my lunch hour, I shouted and bolted outside to the honking carpool—leaping out of my loose shoes.

Ever since the army I've worn shoes a size and a half too large to foil Sergeant Maypop who always ordered my shoes a size and a half too small.

With no laces, the shoes fell off about every two yards, and I had to walk back and start over. Only by clinching my toes and walking very stiff legged, as if on stilts, could I make much headway and even then I was 15 minutes late getting up the street and into the lobby of the office. My progress, with the dropped shoes, looked like a crime diagram showing by footprints which way the criminal went.

I was waiting for the elevator, which had gone off to see its cousin at a bank in Dubuque, when up strolled the managing editor, a kindly man, but I had a hunch he wouldn't approve of his reporter's shoes falling off right and left.

Not at all in the tradition of the free and responsible press. It would have smashed things, if just as Stanley was approaching Livingston to shake hands he had walked out of his shoes.

As we got on the elevator, I forgot to scrooch the old toes, and the shoes remained behind in the lobby, one cocked over the other in a drunken, insolent leer.

Why are you humming so loudly, Friddell? asked the managing editor.

Was I humming? I asked, trying to pull my sock feet up in my trouser legs as I've seen chickens do.

Are you upset over anything? he asked, peering at me.

Au contraire, I replied, trying to hold his eyes to keep him from seeing the shoes out front or my sock feet down below.

The elevator doors shut, we rode up chatting of this and that, and I figured the shoes and socks had gone unnoticed. Later in the day the city editor got a memo from the managing editor to please see that Friddell wears shoes, at least on entering and leaving the building.

# SUBURBIA'S SIBERIA

Like Daniel Boone, moving West when he heard a rooster, today's pioneer flees ever deeper into suburbia. The trouble is, every morning he has to get up and GO BACK into the city.

Furthermore, he goes back in the close confines of a carpool with five of his fellows. It's a little like being in the army twice a day.

Over a period of months they get to know as much about his habits as his family does.

In OUR company carpool, there's a fellow who HUMS when he gets mad. When he starts humming, LOOK OUT! Particularly Tannhauser.

Once you get in a carpool, you never get out. Oh, sure, some people try. The photo editor is trying to get out of our carpool right now, emboldened by the free use he has of the family car all summer.

I'm going in early tomorrow, he says, nervously. Don't pick me up.

Or: I won't be riding this morning. I've got to work late.

We nod . . . and wait . . . until September when his wife has to drive in TWO neighborhood carpools to get the children to school. He'll be back.

One of our members—the aviation editor—was so determined to get out that in the dead of winter he bought a bicycle.

An ENGLISH bicycle.

With a gear for going uphill.

Two mornings we passed him, pedaling furiously, head bent, into the wind. We even cheered as we passed. The third morning he was back with us.

A spoke broke, he said.

The carpool has given me some inkling of what it would be like to live in a socialized society. In Siberia.

Back in February, when I had a nagging cough, out of the blue came a call from my doctor's secretary to say he would see me that afternoon.

Uncanny, I thought. A clear example of ESP. What won't doctors master next!

My doctor rapped and tapped on me, as if looking for a hidden beam on which to hang a picture, found it, and prescribed a cure. On the way out I paused and remarked, casually, to the secretary: Just like my wife to set up an appointment and forget to tell me.

Oh, no, she said. It wasn't your wife. A gentleman in your carpool called.

My car, too, has come up with mysterious coughs, and wheezes. Planned obsolescence, I say. The car is only 15 years old.

Only a couple of more years, said a carpool member, and you can get an antique license.

That hurt. Even the car shuddered at the unkind cut. I took it Saturday for a checkup. The repairman rapped and tapped and at last looked up with the same grave expression I'd seen on the doctor's face.

Mister, he said, there's only one thing wrong with this car.

What's that?

It's TIRED.

He and I just about concluded a deal for a '53 model, a larger car, subject to a tryout.

But on the way to work I mentioned it, off-hand, to the carpool.

Oh, no, Friddell, said the staff artist firmly. You can't buy a car like that. Repairs would eat you up.

You'd better let US pick out your car, said the photo editor.

I have yet to win an argument in the carpool.

This morning there was a free-wheeling discussion of the new Soviet satellite, just up, that weighs $4\frac{1}{2}$ tons.

Big as a couple of cars, said the education editor

Bigger than a small truck, said the staff artist.

Big as a bus, I said, happy I could top them.

A minute later we drew up alongside a bus as it was pulling away from a light, and the staff artist leaned out and bellowed: HEY, BUDDY, HOW MUCH DOES THAT THING WEIGH?

Nine tons, yelled the surpised driver.

Wrong again, Friddell, said the staff artist, leaning back, closing his eyes, wearily.

# POPCORN AT NAVARONE

The Chief was telling what each had to do in blowing up the guns of Navarone—this man captain the expedition, that one be the sharp-shooter, this fellow over here prepare the explosives when suddenly the 6-year-old said he'd like some popcorn, please.

It came as a jolt because I'm the sort that moves right into a movie and there hadn't been any popcorn on the table when we gathered to look at maps and get orders from the Admiral. I had more or less settled down to being Gregory Peck.

Those six destroyers have got to get through, said the Admiral, which means that you've got to get those guns at Navarone, though you haven't a chance, poor devils!

There was crashing music with trumpets, and a voice saying: Guybo, can I go get some popcorn?

This is no time to be thinking of popcorn, I barked. Who let you in here anyway?

That's your son, said my wife, the youngest. All he wants is some popcorn.

In the lobby a throng milled around the popcorn counter. What would Gregory Peck do about THIS? Wait his turn, I bet, like anybody. Sweat it out.

When we got back, Gregory and the boys were running across a strange countryside, chased by Nazis, and the Major was on a stretcher.

What happened? I asked my wife.

Crossed the ocean, climbed a cliff, nothing much.

How 'bout the Major?

Slipped.

Oh.

In the next few minutes it became clear—I saw it even before Gregory—that a member of the underground, a young girl, was spilling information to the Nazis. We were debating what to do with her. David Niven was insisting that we—I—should shoot her, which I didn't much like when somebody said, right in my ear: Guybo, can I have some jelly jubeys?

Jelly WHAT?

Jubeys.

It was the 8-year-old.

Go get your own jelly jubeys.

He can't without disturbing the whole row, whispered my wife.

That was true. Mine were seated in the middle of one full row. I was in an almost empty row in front of them.

Up the aisle at a gallop. Get those jelly jubeys and save that girl, by George. Don't care if she is a spy.

But back at my seat, the girl was gone from the screen.

What happened to Anna? I asked my wife.

I can't tell you.

Why not?

I closed my eyes.

Niven and I managed to get down in the bowels of the fort, right under the guns, where the ammunition was stored, big ugly eggs, but a pack of the enemy was seconds away, cutting through the steel doors with acetylene torches.

We'll never make it, I thought.

I'm dying of thirst, said my wife. Why not get drinks for all of us?

No time to argue. Up the aisle and out to the soft drink machine, racing against time, plugging dimes into the slots, cups rattling down, need more change, throw in a quarter, clunk—KA-ROOM-BOOMEDY-BOOM! from inside.

Well, I thought, anyway we got the guns.

---

# LIONS, TIGERS, AND CANDIED APPLES

When a circus comes to town, whatever money I've got, goes. Fortunately, it is never enough to set off an inflationary cycle, just a momentary flutter in Wall Street when aerodynamics kicks off three or four points, and the wiser heads mutter, Don't buy, don't sell. Just sit tight. Friddell's at the circus.

If we go this time, said my wife, will you promise not to stuff yourself?

I swore not to spend one penny on myself, and, with that, we went.

First there was the animal tent and the elephants, big old Pagliaccis with great moist patches around their eyes, their gray, wrinkled hides about two sizes too large, even for them, groping for handouts.

There went four bags of peanuts, well, three to be precise, since every fourth peanut went down Friddell. But I bought them for the elephants.

Inside the big top, the oldest boy didn't want his hot dog because it had onions, so I ate it, the middle boy asked me to finish his popcorn, large size, the youngest handed me his raspberry snowball, and NOBODY liked the candied apples.

Any minute I expected to hear the ringmaster blare: And up there on the back row, la-dees and gentlemen, about to fall out, is THE HU-MAN GARBAGE PAIL!

You ever try to eat one candied apple and hold two, all three running down your shirt-front? For a show, it beat the fire eater or the sword swallower.

We've got our own freak right here in the stands with us, grumbled the fellow in front of me, a sorehead.

It took Clyde and his cats to divert the attention of those around me. Earlier I'd talked with Beatty as he sunned out back in a canvas chair, great clefts in his chest and thighs where they had come for him—"three months for this, and two months for this one here."

Why do you stay in it? I asked him, and he replied with a memorable line: I'm too old to give it up now.

It's my work, he added, and I like it. We're the only big tented circus left on the road. When I started in 1923 there were at least 20 big railroad circuses.

He's a brown, muscled chunk of a man, built more along the lines of one of his stubby, heavy-chested lions than the sinewy tigers. He has a face like a big, closed fist, strong, square-cut, white teeth in a wide mouth, dark, slit eyes, flat nose, and wiry, curly, black hair.

People think there's a lot of brutality, he went on. There isn't. The quarters are open to the public. You can't hurt 'em. I defy anybody to get in the cage and hurt 'em. It's just patience and knowing each animal. Each cat is different. I don't use any born in captivity. When they're raised among people and see 'em all the time, they get used to 'em.

All the time he was talking, he was jiggling his knee, closing and unclosing his fist. He spoke in spurts. Make sure that meat's got bone in it, he yelled. I don't want no soft meat for my cats.

Once I saw Beatty put his square compact face within an inch of a lion's and match him scowl for scowl for a long 30 seconds, both of them bristling with packed, tawny fury, until suddenly the lion looked away, indifferently, and Beatty sprang back, daintily, cracking his whip.

You can only go so far with them, you know, he told me. If you show the least sign of fear, they detect it very quickly, quicker than a horse or a dog. Never show fear.

I promised I wouldn't. In fact, I promised myself that I wouldn't get close enough to show ANYTHING. Up there in the stands, I watched as Beatty danced about the big cage, a moving, dazzling white spot among the great brown beasts.

In the excitement, I drank my wife's soda pop.

## LEAVE IT TO MAYPOP

The first we knew of Sergeant Maypop was his voice. Some 400 of us had been dumped on a Texas plain, and we stood beneath lavish yellow stars that looked as if you could reach up and peel them off the dark blue ceiling.

Somewhere in the cold dawn a newsboy yelled: "The war's over!" and then as some of us caught our breaths, he added: "All over the world!" Right after that apocalyptic cry came the bellow that was to deafen, if not gladden, our ears for the next four years.

MY NAME IS MAYPOP. I DON'T KNOW WHAT I'VE DONE TO DESERVE YERS, BUT I WILL DO MY BEST TO MAKE YERS WORTHY OF YERS COUNTRY, YERS MOTHERS, AND ME.

We were all 4-F's, and when Maypop saw us in the broad light of day, he decided to re-make us in the image of Government Issue.

He ran us through every inspection the army ever devised. One day he marched the outfit to the camp dental center and then he stalked up and down the aisles, peering over the dentists' shoulders, advising them to pull that one, doc, or fill this, and, why don't yers men brush your teeth more often?

A dozen had teeth in such disrepair that the doctors judged they should be fitted with complete dentures and pulled out ALL their teeth while Maypop held down the indignant men.

It's all fer yers own good, he said. Just leave it to Maypop.

The dental center had just opened, so the impressions for the new teeth had to be sent away somewhere beyond the land of Oz, and before the dentures came back, the outfit was shipped out, the beginning of an odyssey in which the outfit was bounced all over the country, from camp to camp, and then overseas, always just ahead of the dentures.

Maypop fretted as much as the toothless ones. Under a bulky file labeled "False Teeth" he carried on correspondence in triplicate with a dozen camp commanders across the United States, seeking to locate the wandering dentures.

He always put the dentureless dozen at the head of the chow-line. On one Pacific island, when the cooks ran out of ALL food, Maypop consold the teethless ones: At least yers will be the first to get nothing to eat.

Finally, four years later, he made one last effort in a letter that started like this:

To: The President of the United States.

From: Sergeant Maypop.

Subject: False teeth, the lack of.

It may mean my stripes, said Maypop, but I cannot stand it another minute watching yers men try to eat without teeth.

A month later a package about the size of a shoe-box came in the mail, and a minute later Maypop bolted out of his tent, blowing his whistle until his eyes bulged. We fell out in disarray.

Is the war ended? called somebody.

Better than that, bawled Maypop. The teeth are here!

Amid vast cheers the toothless ones stepped forward as May-pop bellowed their names to the skies. They held their new, gleaming dentures out before them as if presenting arms.

Don't yers make a move with those teeth til I give the word, roared Maypop. This is a great moment of my life, and I won't have yers spoil it . . . Now . . . All together . . . Get set . . . TEETH IN!

The dozen jammed in their dentures, and stood there, making painful faces, working their mouths, almost crying.

The teeth didn't fit.

---

## MAYPOP'S AQUACADE

My outfit was formed — using the word loosely — of about 400 4-F's and Sergeant Maypop.

There were men plagued with flat feet, asthma, fallen arches, ulcers, over-weight, deficient hearing, trick knees, bum eyes, and just plain old age.

When we "fell out" for the first formation, we like never to have got up again. It looked like an audition for "The Beggars' Opera."

The Fighting 4-F's we called ourselves, "fighting to get out."

But every time the army, embarrassed at what it had wrought, tried to break the outfit up, the 4-F's fought to stay in.

It's like being told to get up and leave in the middle of a movie, explained Sergeant Maypop. Yers wants to stay and see how it all turns out. Thus far, he added, it has been nothing but comedy, comedy, comedy, but maybe before it's over, yers will do something to make me proud of yers.

Usually it was the machiavellian Maypop who found a way around the army's orders to go home.

One day he called us together and asked how many could not swim. Half the outfit raised its hands.

The army has ordered all yers non-swimmers to go home, he said. In three days I want to see everybody in this mad outfit SWIMMING. Pick a buddy and teach him how to get across the pool and back and don't waste time on fancy strokes.

We did a lot in three days, but at least a quarter of us couldn't swim over and back, and we told the sergeant so.

Don't bother me with details, said Maypop. When the time comes, just get in there and TRESH around.

The day of the swimming inspection, Sergeant Maypop lined all the non and partial swimmers on one side of the pool and all the swimmers on the other.

When the camp commandant arrived, we were all poised on the edge. We LOOKED like swimmers, anyway.

Are they all going to take the test at once, Sergeant? asked the commandant.

That's how it will be if the boat sinks, sir, said Maypop.

You're right, said the commandant. Sergeant Maypop blew a blast on his whistle and all of us plunged into the pool.

It was like the fountains of Versailles gone berserk.

Those who could swim across and back, did, laboring, blowing like whales. The partial swimmers swam out as far as they could, then turned around, and the more expert swimmers coming from the other side, assisted them back to shore. The non-swimmers just stayed at the edge and treshed around as the Sergeant said.

A dozen of the very best swimmers just swam steadily back and forth across the pool, submerging now and then to come up at different spots. On shore, Sergeant Maypop blew continually on his whistle and waved his arms in front of the commandant's face, interfering as much as he could with the commandant's vision.

After about 20 minutes, the commandant yelled, That's enough! Call it off! CALL-IT-OFF!

And get your hands out of my face, Sergeant, he added, OR I'LL BREAK YOU ON THE SPOT.

It took us half an hour to get out of the water. There were splendid feats of life-saving. Then we all lay around the pool, panting. The most spent were the experts.

Maypop, said the commandant, somewhere along the line you are going to run into somebody who is going to break up this crazy outfit and send it home where it belongs, but I'm not man enough to do it.

The commandant started away, then turned and called to the sergeant: One man in there deserves a three-day pass. He swam that pool THIRTY - THREE TIMES.

# HOW TO TAKE DOWN A TREE

There's one thing I refuse to do around the house—well, actually, there are THREE HUNDRED things but there was one this morning—take down the Christmas tree. I agree with what Shakespeare wrote about taking down the Christmas tree when he had Macbeth or Julius Caesar say to Lady Macbeth: If 'tis done, then when 'tis done, 't'were well it were done quickly and while I'm out of the house.

It's such a confounded dispiriting task, as if a brilliant moth were going back to a cocoon. As I write this, my wife is home unwinding the lights, removing the icicles, putting away the ornaments in facial tissues, wrapping up a year, really, taking the trappings to the attic.

Last night, at the request of the 7-year-old, the romanticist in the family, I left the tree lights on and his door half-open until he went to sleep so that the flickering bulbs cast aurora borealis lights across his ceiling and the tree branches threw wierd dancing Byzantine shadows.

This morning all the bounce had gone from its branches, a limp, trailing Blanche du Bois. Even the ornaments seemed tired and a little tawdry in the brisk new year. There's no place for a Christmas tree in the cold realities of January.

So take it down quickly, almost absent-mindedly, as if dusting a chair, I advised her, and only when the tree is leaning by the back gate, allow yourself to say, "It was the best we ever had."

---

# TO MAC'S FRIEND, JOHN SHANDS

The 7-year-olds are inclined to be the quiet ones of this world, full of gravity and deep questions at unexpected moments.

My own has a half-dozen friends with whom he began school, and they have an awareness and understanding of each other that

I do not remember from my own childhood.

They call each other up and in brief conversations which seem to consist mostly of yep and nope conclude business impossible for an elder eavesdropper to get.

Who was that? you ask.

John.

And what did he want?

To talk to me.

In their shy self-sufficiency they remind me of a circle of bright-capped little mushrooms in the lee of a big log or a flock of small birds, flying at the shift of the wind, or cubs rolling in laughter on the lawn.

My own will advance a startling opinion at the supper table and when his older brother asks him, scornfully, who told him THAT, he replies, in serene faith, Roger or Henry or Tommy, as if quoting Einstein.

In a single day I have heard them discuss: What is infinity? ... What does a grasshopper eat?

One of the liveliest of them—and certainly the gentlest—was a child whom you sensed quickly was the product of the finest parents.

He lost his life the other day in an accident at which you can only grieve helpessly for all those involved,

Suddenly it is as if the community were one family.

I have never seen a happier child, living at such a steady pitch of delight, with never a mean word.

His mother, a perfect housekeeper, would simply give her boy and his playmates the run of her home. His father would push aside a pile of business papers to set up Fort Apache.

I've gone to pick up mine and found the two boys, after a day of romping through the house and garden, sunk quietly, dreamily in the same chair ... or lying on their stomachs on the floor, their feet in the air, turning the pages of a book together.

Such notice as this is usually given by newspapers to the older persons of this world. Perhaps these words do not seem proper to you.

I simply wished to pay my respects to the near perfect sweetness of character in one 7-year-old.